EVERYTHING YOU EVER WANTED TO KNOW ABOUT

BUSINESS OTSUKIAI

EVERYTHING YOU EVER WANTED TO KNOW ABOUT

BUSINESS OTSUKIAI

A Guide to Japanese Business Protocol

Translated & Edited by
JAMES V. REILLY

First Printing 1991
Second Printing 1991
Third Printing 1996

Based on the original Japanese language *Business Otsukiai*, compiled and published by NTT Mediascope Inc., copyright 1990.

Translated by James V. Reilly

Edited by HCI and James V. Reilly

Designed by HCI/New York

Illustrations and Cover Design by Peter Müller

Library of Congress Catalog Card Number: 90-64432
ISBN: 0-9628775-0-6

Published and Distributed By:
HCI Publications, Ltd.
275 Madison Avenue, Suite 1801
New York, NY 10016-1101
Tel: 212-922-0199/800-472-1666
Fax: 212-557-5975
e-mail: hciny@aol.com
Internet: http://www.hci-gg.com/hcibooks

Printed and Bound by Port City Press
Printed in the United States of America

FOREWORD

The broad subject matter of this little book is *otsukiai*, a fascinating Japanese term that is often inadequately translated as "associating with" or "friendship," but actually describes the intricate process of building and maintaining all the business and social relationships that are necessary to one's daily life.

Business Otsukiai is about how to get along within Japanese business society—pleasing your superiors, motivating your subordinates, avoiding social and business faux pas, skillfully advancing your career without obviously stepping on others' toes and handling emergencies with tact and the proper decorum.

Deliberately avoiding the academic, analytical approach, the book speaks directly to people who need an intimate acquaintance with Japanese institutions to conduct their business. In it, you'll find many of the lessons that Japanese employees learn by a process of trial and error in the informal classroom of the office, under the guidance of seasoned managers.

Compiled by the staff of NTT Mediascope, a publishing subsidiary of Nippon Telegraph and Telephone Corporation, *Business Otsukiai* is based on a series of formal and informal interviews conducted with 102 middle- and upper-level Japanese managers, almost all of whom were male and from large companies. The views they expressed can be considered fairly representative of mainstream thinking in Japanese business.

The managers were asked for advice for new or inexperienced employees in specific types of situations, ranging from simple tasks like the proper way to make appointments to dealing with the complexities of building a consensus for a proposal. To encourage them to speak more freely, all were assured they would be identified by the initial of their last name only, a common convention observed in Japanese publishing.

Their frank opinions and unguarded observations make *Business Otsukiai* a valuable tool for the business person with a serious interest in penetrating the secrets of corporate Japan, as well as for the general reader seeking insights into the human factors behind the extraordinary success of Japanese companies in the postwar era.

CONTENTS

PART 1 DEALING WITH CUSTOMERS AND VISITORS:
WHAT YOU NEED TO KNOW IF YOU WANT PEOPLE TO RELY ON YOU

PART 2 INSIDE THE COMPANY

PART 3 SECRET TECHNIQUES FOR EXPANDING BUSINESS RELATIONSHIPS

PART 4 CEREMONIES ARE THE PEAK FOR OTSUKIAI — DO YOUR BEST TO MAKE THEM SPECIAL

PART 5 A SHORT COURSE IN GENERAL AFFAIRS KNOW-HOW: LEARN FROM THE PROS

PART 6 AN ILLUSTRATED GUIDE TO OTSUKIAI

PART 1

DEALING WITH CUSTOMERS AND VISITORS

WHAT YOU NEED TO KNOW IF YOU WANT PEOPLE TO RELY ON YOU

CHAPTER 1

APPOINTMENTS

When Asking for Someone's Time, Be Polite

☛ Once it's clear you have to meet, call for an appointment — even if the time and place haven't been decided.

☛ As a rule, *you* should make all the calls for the appointment if it's going to be your first meeting.

☛ Good manners require that you ask the other person whether the time and place for the meeting are convenient.

☛ Sometimes you may need to contact an important executive or other well-known figure. Go ahead with the contact only after finding out who is the right person to go through first.

☛ Always get the name of the other person's colleagues or secretary — just in case.

☛ Never break an appointment. It's also extremely impolite to cut short the time for the meeting or to leave in the middle.

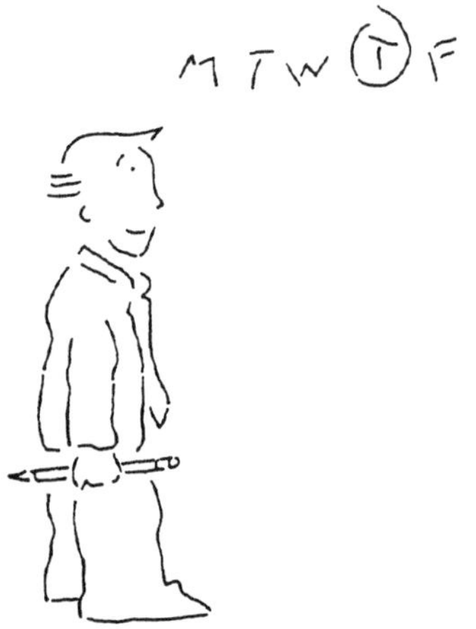

The Time to Make the Appointment is When You First Think You May Need to Meet the Other Person

In business, courtesy requires that appointments for meetings should be made a week in advance. Even when people routinely meet at each other's companies, it's still important to leave at least a day between the request and the meeting itself. And when the meeting time can't be set at that moment, it's always best to ask that the other person hold a certain day open just in case. That way you can call the afternoon before to set the time and not create the impression that you're being sudden and unreasonable. The secret to making appointments successfully is always letting people know as far in advance as possible. And that can also be the secret that will lead to success in your job, too.

When you absolutely need to meet someone fast, it's all right to ask for an hour of their time the following day. But, unless you are extremely busy, you should be flexible enough to meet at whatever time the other person specifies.

Considerations for the First Meeting

When you want to meet someone for the first time on a business matter you wish to propose, first think of the right time to call the person. That time probably will be different for each company, but, in general, around 10 a.m. is best.

☛ When the right person gets on the line, first tell him who you are, and then ask if you can speak to him for about five minutes. After he agrees, briefly tell him the nature of your business, ask what time is most convenient for him and then adjust your schedule to it. Even when it's urgent that you meet someone, you should be ready to offer several different options for the meeting time.

☛ When the person you wish to speak with is not at his desk, ask someone to tell him that you will call again later.

☛ When the other person has to come to your company, be sure to send a map of the route to him either by fax or by mail, and also send your business card. To make it easier for him to contact you also write on the card the name of someone he can speak to when you're away from your desk.

When Problems Come Up

☛ When you're meeting outside the office, it's best to provide a number at which you can be contacted. Also, if the meeting is to take place in a public place, like a train station or public building, always arrive five minutes before the appointed time.

☛ When it looks as if you'll be late for an appointment, always call the other person's office. If it seems that you'll be ten minutes late, for example, then it's best to say you'll be 15 minutes late. That five minutes of margin will probably be necessary. And if you actually manage to make it to the appointed place only ten minutes late, then the other person will probably take it as a sign of your sincerity that you came in such a hurry you shaved five minutes off your time.

Appointments People Make

When inviting a VIP to give a speech at our bank, we always write a letter first. We invite the person to speak about a certain subject at a particular time, and also specify the desired length of the speech. We enclose our corporate brochure, information about past speakers we've invited and other materials. Only then do we make a telephone call to him. If we didn't handle the contact this way, we couldn't get a clear answer on whether the person would accept our invitation.
— Bank Manager

Construction companies arrange to meet their customers in coffeehouses near major railroad stations. Since we often have to meet customers for the first time in such places, we have to do something so they'll recognize us. I usually place a stack of our corporate literature on the table, so I always carry a few brochures with me.
— Construction Company Sales Executive

CHAPTER 2

YOUR COMPANY'S FIRST IMPRESSION

Showing Visitors In and Out is a Chance to Develop Business

☛ A visitor watches everything that goes on in the company. All employees should greet visitors crisply and bow when meeting them.

☛ Make a visitor feel that you have been looking forward to meeting him.

☛ When showing a visitor around your company, be reserved but smile and never turn your back towards him. Always be sure to personally escort him when he has to go to another building or someplace else that may be difficult for an outsider to find.

☛ Don't ever let anyone feel that they're not being given the fullest courtesy in a meeting or reception room. Be sure to keep the doors to all other reception rooms closed.

☛ If you see a visitor who looks as if he's waiting for someone, politely inquire whether you can help him.

☛ There's a tendency for some people to look very serious when seeing a guest out. Keep a friendly patter going until you see the person out of your office to the elevator.

☛ Seeing a visitor out of your office is a good chance to remind him of another matter of importance or to ask a favor. Don't miss the opportunity.

A Sharp Person Can Make Up His Mind about a Company from What He Hears Employees Whispering to Each Other in the Halls

Always Be Conscious That How You Look and Behave Reflects on Your Company!

Mr. T, the assistant to the president of a certain large company, makes it a practice—whenever his boss is to visit the president of another company—to drop by their offices several times on the pretext of making arrangements for the meeting.

The real objective in doing this is to decide whether the other company would be a good partner to do business with or not.

"It's only proper that the general affairs person or the special assistant to the president at that company will be very courteous," he explained. "But I make it a point to talk to young employees I see in the corridors. I'll inquire about how to get to another office in the building, for example. How they answer gives me a good idea about the state of employee training and the atmosphere in the company. I also listen to catch what they whisper among themselves. This tells a lot about the quality of employees."

Many visitors come to your offices. Among them will be some who can determine the fate of the company. Welcoming guests is not just the job of the receptionist: there must be an attitude that the whole company welcomes the visitor.

☛ Inform the receptionist ahead of time that you are expecting a guest, giving him or her the visitor's name and the time of the appointment. When the receptionist shows your visitor he is expected, it makes for a warmer welcome.

☛ Reserve a conference room in advance if you plan to have a meeting. Make sure that all other conference room doors are closed. This avoids giving the impression that there are better conference rooms than the one you'll be meeting in.

☛ Don't leave the visitor stranded in the reception area. There should be a sofa for visitors to sit on and magazines and company brochures for them to read. Visitors waiting near the entrance should be asked if they need help.

☛ When coming upon visitors in the corridors, be sure to bow.

After showing important visitors or older people to conference or meeting rooms, ask what they would care to drink.

Tips

- ***Be as polite as possible.***
- ***As a rule, the person receiving the guest should always stay on the right. Going up the stairs, the person showing the way is in front. Going down, the visitor is in front.***
- ***Getting on the elevator, the person showing the way enters first and keeps the door open for the visitor. Getting off, the visitor goes first. When there is an elevator operator, the visitor boards first and gets off after the person showing the way.***

Mr. O, a secretary to the head of one of Japan's most powerful government ministries, tells this story:

"Whenever the Minister visited companies in the middle of summer, the air conditioning would invariably be turned all the way up. As his secretary, it fell to me to make sure that he was never served the usual cold drinks. Whenever I found cups of deliciously brewed hot tea waiting for us in a chilly conference room in July or August, I thought to myself, `Now here's a company that knows what it's doing.' "

Whenever an important visitor is scheduled to come to the office, it's essential to go over all the details with your boss in advance.

Seeing Visitors Out

"The first time, I was shown out to the elevator, and the next time only as far as the receptionist. It makes you feel like you're not that important anymore."

Even if you think that by now you've become close enough to dispense with formalities, the visitor might not feel the same way. The best way is to *always* see visitors out the same way. Decide how far you will see people out — to the reception desk, to the elevator or best of all to their car — and don't change it.

Also, when you see your guests as far as the elevator, in that minute or so until the elevator comes, use the chance productively to thank them for the useful discussion, bring their attention to a matter of importance or encourage them. Above all, don't run off to other things without properly ending the visit.

CHAPTER 3

MEETING VISITORS: MAKE THEM FEEL THEY'RE NUMBER ONE

☛ Run through the final checklist ten minutes before the meeting: Coffee and tea ready? Ash trays? Materials all in place?

☛ When the visitor arrives, chat for awhile about general topics and create a pleasant mood.

☛ When more than one person is meeting with a guest, it's best if everyone knows the agenda along which the discussion will progress.

☛ Your attitude should be: "The customer is always right." Your attention to the small details tells a lot about your company's sensitivity to the visitor.

☛ Visitors who arrive without notice can also lead to business. Treat them very courteously.

☛ During your meeting, make the visitor feel he's the most important person you know. Don't leave the room or take phone calls unless it's absolutely necessary.

☛ There is a flow to meetings. Leading the flow carefully can produce results.

The Feeling is: "We're Honored to Have You Visit Us."

Preparation Begins as Soon as You Set the Time for the Meeting

Everything is going well until you show the very important visitor into the conference room. There on the table are ashtrays brimming with ashes and cigarette butts and dirty coffee cups that haven't been cleared away yet. And on top of it all, the air in the room is stale and stifling. As you throw the window open, you pick up the phone to call to have someone come into the conference room to pick things up. But no matter how much you try to recover, the damage is done. The visitor doesn't have quite the same impression of your company.

It's only common sense that conference rooms should always be kept clean. Reserve the room ahead of time and then shortly before the meeting check to make sure everything is ready: tea or coffee, ashtrays and air conditioning. When documents are to be used at the meeting make sure that enough copies for everyone attending are made and placed in the room ahead of time.

Set a Pleasant Tone to Meetings

Rather than start with the main topic as soon as the visitor is seated, you can create a more pleasant mood by first chatting a little about unrelated matters. Look at this phase of the meeting as a kind of warm-up for the actual business talk to come.

Coffee and tea should be served with the right timing. There are those who will turn to a subordinate at a meeting and tell him to fetch tea. But it's better to ask someone who will not be at the meeting to serve beverages. This tells your visitors that each person at the meeting, even the lowliest new employee, has his or her own important function to play.

More Than One is Better

Even if there is only one visitor, it's best to have several people from your company meet him. If several people can report on the conclusions reached and the progress of negotiations, it's possible for the company to avoid making a bad judgement based on the comments of one person.

Also, having a number of people to meet the visitors means they can handle all the functions that may come up in the meeting, including the helper who'll go to fetch necessary documents that are not in the room; the controller who'll prevent anyone from getting way ahead of the others at the meeting; and the mood maker who sets the appropriate feeling for the conference.

Having several people meet can also be desirable when dealing with complaints from outside the company, or when uninvited visitors turn up.

Introduce Everyone

Make sure that everyone who attends the meeting is properly introduced, even the lowest-ranking new employee. Introducing your subordinates makes it easier for them to speak up if they have to. But remember to keep the introductions brief and to the point.

A key part of the introduction is to let the visitor know to whom he can speak, and at what telephone extension, when you are out of the office.

Fruitful Meetings That End on Time

After completing the preliminaries, the job is to conclude as much business as possible and reach agreement within the time allotted for the meeting. As the meeting proceeds, keep in mind how the meeting is moving and whether the appropriate amount of time is being given to each item on the agenda. If time is running short, briefly cover all of the main points and summarize as much as necessary.

"You Are a Very Important Person to Our Company."

Skillfully Staging the Flow of the Meeting

If the Mood of the Meeting Turns Sour, Change It!

If the visitor starts leafing through documents when there's no need to or suddenly grows silent, the mood of the meeting can become strained. You can change the course of the meeting at this point by bringing up another aspect of the discussion or relating an interesting episode that is somehow related to the issue at hand. In using this tactic, be careful not to get carried away with what you are saying and forget about focusing on what's going on in the visitor's mind.

When You Want to Make a Note of the Important Points in the Conversation

You're dutifully listening to a visitor's presentation. As his remarks turn to another subject, your expression changes, you whip out your pen and begin taking notes. Not surprisingly, the

Ceremonial Visits are for Business, Too

"There are times when appointments are made for people to visit your office and you have no idea what will be discussed or why the visitor has requested the meeting," says Mr. S, an executive in a large securities house in Tokyo. "There is such a thing as a ceremonial visit, and such visitors have to be treated with due respect and courtesy. You never know whether the meeting might develop into important business someday."

There are also surprise visits for which no appointment has been made. There can be no excuse for not showing your face, or having a receptionist tell the visitor you are in a meeting, or that you've never heard of them. That's the same as slamming the door in the caller's face. People get angry when you make them lose face. When someone visits without an appointment, by all means receive him warmly.

visitor feels that nothing he has said up to this point has struck you as worth recording. In other words, everything he has said until now has been wasted on you.

Mr. M, the head of general affairs at a trading company, gives this advice about taking notes: "Make sure you have a pad with you from the very start of the conversation. In addition to jotting down the main points, take notes at other phases in the conversation." This is helpful because it keeps the other person guessing at what your company finds of most interest.

When Someone Calls the Boss While He is Receiving a Visitor

Of course, the best response is to say that he is busy receiving a visitor and will call back later. But when it is an urgent matter, you can give him a message. Of course, while the visitor is talking you can not pass your boss a note without giving offense.

If you have to break into the conversation, wait until your boss is speaking to the visitor, and then pass him the note. At the same time, be sure to ask the visitor to forgive the intrusion. You always want to convey the message to the visitor that he is very important to your company. If you take calls often, though, you can give the impression that the company doesn't care about the visitor at all.

Of course, no one expects every business meeting will result in a deal. But whether or not the visitor leaves with his feelings intact will have repercussions long after the meeting is over. Receiving a visitor as you would like to be received will improve your image and that of your company in the visitor's eyes.

Receiving Visitors with the Right Touch

"You can never spend enough time training employees to serve customers properly," explains Mr. K, a veteran executive in the employee training department of a major department store. "We train our employees, for example, to walk three paces behind the customer."

Giving this kind of attention to the small details results in a level of service that always leaves the customer with a positive feeling. To touch the customer's heart demands attentive service that doesn't overlook any of the details.

Preparing Things for Visitors Properly

There is a proper way to give things to visitors at meetings:

☛ take the cap off the pen so that the visitor can use it right away;

☛ if the visitor asks for a scissors, don't pass it point first, and;

☛ when documents or books are being shown, make sure that there are tabs on them to make it easy to find the relevant sections.

Another Cup?

If you have served your guest a cup of coffee at the start of the meeting, it's often useful to offer another cup when you start talking about the main issue of the meeting. Whether he accepts or not, your visitor will appreciate the kindness you've shown.

Using Your Wits Can Make You Shine a Hundred Times Brighter

When a Manager Can't Come to Meet the Visitor Right Away

Tell the receptionist to let the visitor know that someone from the manager's section will come to meet him shortly. Having done this, don't assume it's all right to keep the visitor waiting indefinitely.

In addition to letting the visitor know how long it will be before the person will come for him, provide a hot beverage and reading materials to make the wait more pleasant.

When the Person Being Visited is Not in the Office

"This often happens," says securities industry executive Mr. M. "If by chance no one knows where the executive has gone it could hurt an outsider's view of our company, so we usually explain that he's in the building but away from his desk at the time. The executive's subordinate or boss will then come out to meet the visitor."

Taking Care of a Visitor's Luggage

Sometimes visitors who are travelling on business will be carrying luggage with them. Before formally greeting them, offer to have reception hold their luggage for them.

When the Visitor Has Forgotten Something at Your Company

Estimate how long it will take him to return to his company and then call him yourself. If the person is not there yet, leave word that you called and that you will call him again later. Under no circumstances should you say that you have found what he left behind and wish to return it to him. Being labelled forgetful is a minus factor and could hurt his standing within his company.

Put Visitors' Names on Materials for the Meeting

Place materials with the visitor's name on them on the meeting room table ahead of time. This saves time that would otherwise be spent handing out materials and finding seats. It also makes visitors feel you're more well-prepared to meet them.

CHAPTER 4

BUSINESS CARDS

Will They Be Assets or Mere Scraps of Paper? It's Up to You

☛ Forgot your business card? Don't worry. Mail it tomorrow and leave a stronger impression.

☛ Exchange cards as soon as you meet. Don't wait until you settle down for a formal meeting.

☛ Business cards are an important source of data. Try making a map of the human networks inside your customer's organization.

☛ Good connections inside the company can come in handy. Exchange business cards with people inside your company, too.

☛ A business card is a record of your activities. Jot down the date you met, some details that struck you about the person and keep it for future reference.

☛ When introducing yourself, always give your name before you say what company you represent.

☛ Never keep your business cards in your back pocket.

Otsukiai Begins with a Single Business Card

Mr. K, an executive for an electronics manufacturing company, was to meet an important client when he realized he was out of business cards. This is how he handled the situation:

"I was supposed to have business cards and I didn't. In any case, I apologized on the spot and then sent a short note the following day along with one of my cards. As it happens, it all worked out for the best. I left a stronger impression on the customer, and ever since then we have been working very smoothly with his company."

Mr. K's quick response left his customer with a vivid impression of his sincerity and seriousness of purpose. This is far from what he had expected would happen.

It's More Productive to Start off Your Introduction by Giving Your Own Name First Rather Than Your Company's

The most common way to exchange business cards is to say your company's name first before saying your own name. Mr. A, a bank executive, suggests a better way. "I always give my name first, then say it's nice to meet you and tell the other person I'm from the finance department of my bank," he reports. Mr. A does this because he knows mentioning his name first will leave a lasting impression on the person he's meeting.

In banks and other businesses where the relationship between the executive and the customer is very important, this method seems to be more effective. But whatever the order, the spirit behind exchanging cards is to create a mutual relationship with another person.

Business Cards Can Become Seeds for New Business

Exchange Cards as Soon as You Meet

There are many people who think that it's impolite to initiate an exchange of cards in a busy place, say for example a train station where you have just met the other person. Such people often think that it's better to wait until you reach a place where you can settle down and talk with the other person. But walking to such a place with a person you have not been introduced to can be disconcerting and uncomfortable. Remind yourself that there is no such thing as a place where it's impolite to offer to exchange cards. It's by far much more impolite to meet someone and not immediately offer to exchange cards.

Who Goes First?

When a number of people are to exchange cards, the order starts with the senior persons and proceeds to those less senior. If a higher ranking person from the group you are meeting mistakenly goes to present his card to a lower ranking person from your group, the lower ranking person should be alert enough to step back a bit to let his superior exchange cards first.

Starting Up the Conversation

A veteran of over 20 years in sales tells how he develops the conversation after exchanging cards: "I look at the person's card and ask about the person's name, his department and the origin of the company's name. This helps to break the ice with the other person."

Business Card Trivia

Business Cards Overseas

In Europe and America people don't ordinarily exchange business cards on the first meeting. But recently the value of the business card is being recognized and exchanges of business cards have become quite routine.

Preventing Business Card Abuse

If you're worried about giving your business card to someone whose character you have doubts about, just say that you're sorry you've just run out of cards. Another way to keep people from misusing your card is to write the date or scribble a number on your cards. If something is written on a card, it makes it difficult for anyone to use it for an illegitimate purpose.

It's foolish to exchange cards just to learn each other's names. Exchanging cards marks the starting line of human relationships.

Convenient Name Cards

In America and elsewhere people often use name cards, cards with only the person's name printed on them. In the blank space around the name, a person can write an address or telephone number.

The Business Card: Your Best Source of Data

It's often said that the more business cards you collect the better a business person you are. But you will never know the value of people's cards until you make full use of them.

Added Value Business Cards

Some people's business cards carry a calendar on the back, a table showing the calories in popular foods, mathematical tables, actuarial and other tables. Nothing makes a first conversation easier than giving someone a business card with interesting information related to your work printed on the back.

Make a Map of the Human Networks

Interior decorator Mr. A exchanges cards with everyone he can find at the large department store that's one of his best clients. "I get cards from everyone from the board of directors on down to the lowest ranked new employee," he says. "By doing this I can see who is whose boss, who is whose subordinate and grasp the overall picture of what kind of organization the department store is."

In short, by using business cards, he constructs a map of all the human networks within the company.

Even for people who work in large corporations, these in-company power relationships are important. Mr. S, an employee of a large pharmaceutical company that hires several hundred executives fresh out of universities every year, is a good example. Mr. S visits those in the same entering class he belonged to and has them show him their business card files.

"In particular, I check the files of friends in different sections of the company," he says. "If there is someone in their files I'd like to put in my network, I have them introduce me. Thanks to their help, I have a good network of connections throughout the whole company."

Making Cards a Sales Diary

Sales people who go out and make calls every day collect a great many cards. Over a week's time they receive so many cards, in fact, that they lose track of them. To cope with the problem, it's best to take all the cards you receive and put them in some sort of order as soon as you get back to the company. If you write on the card the reason you met the person plus any impressions, you'll find that it's a lot easier to recall the person's face and other details later on. By filing business cards by the date you receive them and writing notes on them, you can keep a good daily diary of your business activities.

Throwing Them Away

Transport company manager Mr. U gives advice on when to start letting go: "There's probably going to be another time when you'll have to call on the person you worked with five years ago, so I never throw away any cards of people with whom I've worked closely. The cards I do throw away are those from people I either don't remember or have not heard from. I usually go through my cards and weed these out once a year."

They say that if you check an old business card, you can usually find where a person is now. This is why Mr. U takes all of the business cards he wants to keep and stores them with his daily diary for that year. "That way, you know exactly when you met them," he says.

How to Exchange Cards

Your Pocket is Not a Business Card Holder

Offering a business card you've just pulled out of a shirt pocket is impolite. And it's equally offensive to take the card you've just received and pop it into the same pocket. The most unpardonable offense is taking a card out of or placing a card you've received into your back pocket. A business person should, at the very least, have a proper business card holder.

When Someone in a Superior Position Offers His Card While Seated, You Should Stand to Receive It

In a Japanese-style tatami room this may seem a bit exaggerated, so you should straighten your back and sit formally to receive the card.

Give the Card Directly

It is a breach of etiquette to place your card on the table for someone to pick up. It leaves the impression that instead of trying to start a relationship with someone, you're trying to avoid him. In addition to the bad feeling it leaves, the card itself is difficult to pick up off the flat surface of the table.

Bowing is Part of It

Cards are exchanged after the two people have bowed to each other properly. You should be careful not to make a perfunctory bow, say by lowering your head only, since people may take it as an indication of your character as well as the character and level of your company. Nevertheless, be careful not to bow too deeply. When exchanging cards, bows should be crisp and not too low.

Cards Have Multiple Uses

- ***"When someone calls and asks me to send them materials, I always enclose a card. Since I worry that the card will get bent if I clip it to the materials, I usually put it in a small envelope with a brief note written on a buck slip."***
- ***"When I'm sending materials to someone, I usually find a blank spot on the cover letter page and affix my card to it. You can make a little ring out of a piece of tape, keeping the sticky side out, and attach it to the back of the card."***
- ***"When I visit someone and they're out I usually write a message on my card and have someone leave it on their desk. After collecting about five of these, the person will usually meet with you if only because he feels sorry for you."***

Cards for Introductions and Messages

• In the upper left hand corner write the person's name. Below that, ask him to see the back of the card for the favor you want. Write the details on the back of the card and don't forget to either sign it or place your stamp on it.

Widen Your Human Network with Business Cards

If you confine your network building to the business world, you can only reach a limited group of people. But you can also use cards to extend your networks to other worlds as well.

Mr. H, a ham radio enthusiast for more than 20 years, had special cards made with his call sign printed on them. He always carries them along with his business cards.

"After talking for awhile and discovering that the other person is also a ham, I whip out my ham radio cards," he says. "Giving people such cards that have some special theme or interesting or decorative aspect make both people happy and bring you closer through the experience."

Cards with No Titles

Mr. S, the president of a toy company, has cards that show his name but no title. Why break with convention and do away with titles?

"If I go to a pub or a small bar and meet some young people and become friendly with them, it makes things easier to have a card with my name only on it," he says. "Now, if I pulled out a card that said president on it, they'd probably change their tone and become more formal. There'd be lots of things they wouldn't feel free to talk about with me. There are many things I want to ask young people and get an honest answer, and I can't do that unless they're relaxed when they talk with me. If they just think I'm an ordinary old man they'll feel at ease with me. That's why I don't put a title on my cards."

Cards for the Neighborhood

Mr. Y manages a Little League baseball team and carries a card he had printed with his name and the inscription "Hiroshi's father."

"If you're making an effort to communicate through your children," he explains, "then why not put your children's names on your cards. . . Thanks in part to these cards, my campaign to communicate with the local community is going very well and I have made friends I would never have dreamed of in the past."

There are cards for every purpose and people are finding more and more new ways to use them. Whether it's your card or someone else's, you'll want to treat these small scraps of paper that can become either assets or trash as extensions of the person.

CHAPTER 5

TELEPHONE CALLS

Your Voice Tells Enough about You to Be Dangerous

- ☛ Straighten up and smile when talking on the phone. Your voice should be crisp and pleasant.
- ☛ When apologizing on the phone, it's proper to bow.
- ☛ Use the most polite language possible.
- ☛ People are often put off by little things you may say on the phone. Be careful to avoid upsetting them.
- ☛ Be sure to thank those who call from outside as well as those from within the company.
- ☛ When you put someone on hold, and it turns out the called party isn't available, be sure to apologize and explain the situation.
- ☛ Begin your phone calls by asking if you can speak for ten minutes or so about a particular topic. Before proceeding be sure the other person agrees.

To Avoid Unpleasantness on the Phone

"I was in the middle of a phone call and thought I might as well have a cigarette since the conversation was going to take awhile. I lit up and inhaled when suddenly the person on the other end started coughing uncontrollably. 'I'm allergic to cigarette smoke,' he gasped as I hurried to crush it out."

This is one of those truth-is-stranger-than fiction stories that is definitely true. At the sound of the lighter and then the person exhaling smoke the person listening on the other receiver started choking. This indicates what a strong image is transmitted over the telephone wires. Even if you work on polishing your telephone voice alone and not your attitude toward the caller, people will be able to see through you. That's the most frightening aspect of the telephone.

Be Especially Polite When Someone is Out

• When someone from your office is out and can't answer a call, it means that the caller's time is wasted and, to a certain extent, there is a halt in the flow of work at the caller's company. Be sure to be properly apologetic.

• When someone calls back and the called party is still at an outside meeting, be apologetic and explain that the meeting is taking longer than expected. Phrase your explanation in such a way that the caller feels your colleague has not returned because of circumstance over which he has no control.

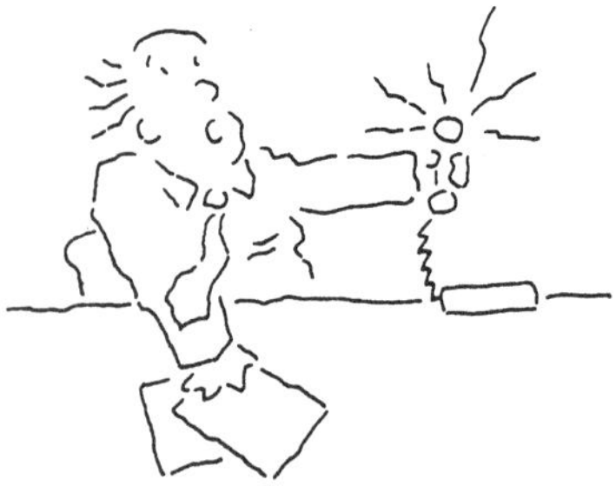

On the other hand, if you can work a little sincerity into your telephone routines, you can make the telephone your most powerful business tool.

Most Unpleasant Telephone Experiences— First Place: "He's Out of the Office"

You call a company and ask if you can speak to a particular person. Yes, he's here, please wait, you are told. And wait you do until finally a voice comes over the line again and tells you that he's out of the office now. "That's funny," you think to yourself, "it sounded like he was there at first." Especially since you heard someone call him just before you were put on hold. Naturally, you wonder if he's trying to avoid you.

We've probably all had this kind of experience. This is why we should be extremely careful on the telephone.

☛ If you don't know for sure, don't answer yes when asked if someone is in the office. The caller will take that to mean that he is definitely in the office. You can say you'll check or that you think he may be in the office, and then ask the caller to wait as you put the call on hold.

☛ When the called party is not available, you should say: "I'm very sorry, I thought he was at his desk, but he's stepped out of the office."

By starting off with "I'm very sorry," you let the caller know that you aren't the one he's trying to call and stop him before he launches into the conversation he planned to have with the person he wanted to speak with first.

☛ To avoid creating misunderstandings on the telephone, write in your destination on the office schedule board if you'll be away from your desk more than 10 minutes.

Most Unpleasant Telephone Experiences— Second Place: Waiting

If the phone rings three times before anyone picks it up, be sure to begin by saying that you're sorry to have kept the caller waiting. If it rings five times, say that you're *very* sorry for the delay. If after being answered the call is transferred but then rings for more than 10 seconds, the switchboard operator should come on the line again and apologize for the delay.

When you have to keep someone on the line while you refer to materials or check on facts, remember that the absolute limit for keeping someone waiting is 30 seconds. If it looks like it'll take longer than that, say you'll call the person back. If the caller offers to wait, then you should keep him waiting on the line no longer than a minute. Waiting a minute with a telephone receiver in your hand feels like waiting five minutes anywhere else.

"I'm in a Hurry"

When someone is obviously in a big hurry, observing all the regular practices for answering the phone may make him irritated. If you sense a strong urgency in someone's voice, dispense with the usual formalities.

Telephone Tag

When someone is not there to talk to the caller, saying he's at a meeting outside and hanging up is not the proper way to respond. It's your duty to ask if the call is urgent or see what the call is in reference to so you can find the right person to help.

Here's an example of how you can respond when someone is not there to answer the phone:

You: Mr.Sato will be back around three o'clock. Shall I have him call you at that time?

Caller: I'll be in a meeting at three. I'll call him back at five.

You: I don't know Mr. Sato's schedule for later this afternoon, so shall I ask him to call you around five.

Caller: Fine. If my meeting runs past five, please tell him to get in touch with Mr. Tanaka here. He knows what this matter is about.

Improving Your Telephone Talk

We're living in a time when everything from the merging of companies to a couple's divorce can be stopped with a single phone call. Here are a few hints to add spark to your telephone conversations:

☛ Straighten up your posture, and try to speak in a slightly higher voice. Speak clearly.

☛ Attune your conversation to the tempo or rhythm of the other person's speaking. This helps eliminate any uneasiness the caller may feel about not being able to see your face.

☛ Put feeling into your gestures. When you tell the other person that you understand his situation, you should put as much

"While You Were Out" Memos

- ***If you write in the time, date and subject on the memorandum, it makes it easier for the person to respond to the call.***

- ***Keep the recorded greeting on your telephone answering machine short and to the point. The caller is already disappointed that you're not on the phone and doesn't want to listen to some long-winded explanation.***

To Prevent Misunderstandings

• ***Confirm numbers by repeating them in different ways. If the other party says one zero six eight, you can confirm by saying one thousand sixty eight.***

• ***When you must use difficult expressions or technical terms, add a few words to help the other person understand them.***

feeling into it as you would if you were not on the phone. You should also nod your head in agreement. Gestures on the phone help to convince the other person of your sincerity.

☛ Before hanging up, try to leave an even better impression. Thank the person for his or her help, and then say you look forward to speaking with them again.

A Good Call Covers All Items on the Agenda

Conversing on the telephone is something that comes naturally, but in the ordinary business call, methodically covering all the items on the agenda is more important than how well you carry on the conversation. This is because you're talking about documents or products without having them there in front of your eyes for both parties to see.

First, you'll want to write out each item you wish to cover in the call so you can check them off as you talk. Then, when you're finished going through them, you and the other person should once again go over the points that remain to be clarified and the problems that still need to be resolved.

For detailed talks, it's necessary to put certain items aside to make sure that progress is made on the main topic of business. When calls take upwards of 20 minutes, it's better to set aside time and meet in person.

SOME TELEPHONE SITUATIONS

Always Have 10 Yen Coins in Your Pocket

You race to make a call from a bank of public phones on the platform where you're changing trains. As soon as you reach them, though, you find all the card phones are in use. You search in your pockets for some change to use in the coin phones but can't find any. You race to the end of the platform, buy a magazine to get change and run back to make the call. By then you know you're already late for your next appointment.

Always make sure you have telephone cards and ten yen coins with you whenever you're out on business.

The Receptionist Turned Out to Be the President

A woman's voice comes on the line just as you are thinking that no one will ever answer your call. "Sorry to have kept you waiting," she says as you grow angrier, "but we were on our lunch hour." You realize then why it has taken so long, but keep up the conversation with the same angry feeling you had about being kept waiting. Later you break out in a cold sweat when you learn that she's the president of the company.

Don't call companies during lunch hour. And remember: *anyone*, including the president and top executives, can pick up a phone that's ringing. Always be polite on the phone.

1

CHAPTER 6

FOR EFFECTIVE CONVERSATIONS

Reach the Top Without Straining

☛ Before you start talking, make a list either on paper or in your head of all the main points to be covered as well as the content of the conversation.

☛ Assume that people can listen without getting bored for about two minutes. Lay out the essentials in a businesslike manner, making frequent pauses to facilitate understanding.

☛ Using examples can enliven your conversation.

☛ To make the talk productive, consider your relationship and distance from the other person in deciding where to focus your eyes, what gestures to use and what tone to take in speaking.

☛ In business, never use crude language or act overly familiar.

☛ A good talker is usually also a good listener. You have one mouth but two ears, so try to do twice as much listening as talking.

☛ Using technical terms and unnecessarily difficult expressions will be taken as merely showing off. Avoid them as much as possible.

Some Believe the Less Said the Better, But Results Don't Happen Until You Start Talking

There are times when it's smart not to say anything. When someone is writing a report furiously after having been reprimanded by a superior, offering a word of sympathy will probably only earn you an angry look.

But conversation is needed for human relationships to work. In the beginning there was the word, the Bible says. When talking, don't just say the first thing that comes to your mind. For a lively conversation, you need to take into account the particular situation, the temperament of the other person and the atmosphere.

Ad agency executive Mr. Z tells this story: "The silent ones are the toughest customers, aren't they? They listen to your presentation looking down at the table, not saying anything. Then just when you're about to give up in disgust and leave, they say okay to what you're proposing. But rather than be happy with that, you're left wishing that they could show some sort of reaction to what you're saying."

Every day is full of deadly serious conversations about business. Silently listening without reacting to what the other person is saying is impolite. "For people who are skillful (but not silent) listeners, you want to do more than an ordinary job," explains Mr. Z "For them, 120% isn't too much."

How can you inspire people to do 120% for you?

☛ Start off by being positive both in what you say and the gestures you use. Tell the other person that what he's saying is true and reasonable, and only then tell him what your position is. Once the other person understands that you respect him, he'll be more willing to accept your wishes.

☛ Every now and then break off from the main topic for a few minutes. Sometimes these pauses can lead to an entirely fresh, new development.

☛ If you want to get someone on your side, sprinkle your conversation with expressions that show you recognize and value his opinion: "I see your point," "That's an excellent observation," or some similar expressions. It's only human to crave recognition and acceptance, and to feel gratified when you receive it. One precaution: if your praise for the other person sounds affected or artificial in any way, the effort will be counterproductive.

How Your Eyes Perform is Also Important

They say the eyes, too, can speak volumes. Think of your eyes as every bit as important as your tongue. Of course, it's best to look someone in the eye when you speak with him, but there are times when this produces unwanted tension. Try to fix your gaze a little below the other person's eyes.

Where you sit, too, can have a lot to do with how the conversation flows. The sketch at the right shows a seating arrangement for a conversation used in a psychology experiment. In this arrangement, C and D were the positions where the most conversation was made. F spoke three times as much with E than with B, who was directly across the table from him. Keep this diagram in the back of your mind, and the next time you have to make a seating chart, put yourself in C, the one you most want to talk with in position D, and the one you'd like to keep at a respectful distance in position F.

Seating Positions and Distances to Keep When Speaking

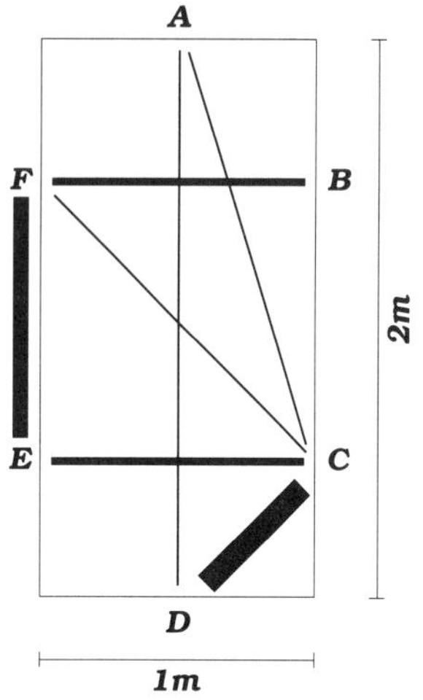

Never Make the Other Person Feel Uncomfortable

When speaking to others in your company about visitors, use the words "gentleman" instead of man and "lady" instead of woman.

☛ Rather than say "I believe you're aware of this already," it's better to leave open the possibility that he or she isn't. Try instead: "Perhaps you may have heard of this already."

☛ When greeting people, some have the aggravating habit of making remarks about how fat one has become or how pale one looks today. Remarks like this are not forgotten and each time they are remembered they are more painful.

☛ If you use expressions like "one of our girls" for a female employee or "one of our vendors," it may be offensive not only to the person about whom it's being said but also to other non-company people who may overhear.

Choose Topics that Have a Fresh, Up-to-Date Feeling

When sitting down to talk business, it's helpful to start off by talking about some bright, upbeat and recent development: Ginza fashions, the latest trends on Tokyo's waterfront project or some other interesting subject. It may take a little time, but it won't hurt to do some research and educate yourself about a certain topic so you can easily speak with authority about it.

Topics to Avoid:

☛ Topics related to politics or religion. When these topics come up people's beliefs or value systems are revealed. It's better to avoid such topics in business.

☛ Rumors about a boss or subordinate, or a related company.

☛ Children's education problems. When the talk turns to ideals of education, personal education stories or complaints about the system, people usually feel uncomfortable.

Pay Attention to the Flow of Things

In business, it's important to leave people with a positive feeling after a meeting. This is why we usually end by telling them the meeting was informative, or you're glad you met with them or that simply you want to meet them again.

Even when a business meeting bogs down and the talk becomes difficult, end on an unemotional note, and give the other person credit for his contribution to the meeting. If you see the conversation running toward a dangerous topic or rumor, you'll want to head it off and direct the flow toward another subject.

Personnel manager Mr. Y puts it this way: "In meetings, there's always someone who will strike the right notes and start the conversation off beautifully. This has nothing to do with age, by the way. I myself like to attend such meetings and observe my subordinates without saying anything. That way I can determine who I can depend on to run meetings in the future." Conversation skills express the person. You can never polish them enough.

The Three Evils of Speech

Tediousness
Repeating the same thing over and over. Going around the issue without ever coming to the point. Bragging about personal things. Running over the allotted time.

Pushiness
Speaking one-sidedly without allowing the other person to put in a word or two or ask questions. "Look, you can't afford to pass up this work, right?" This attitude invites a harsh reaction.

Sarcasm and Offensiveness
When someone says things like "I'm close to your managing director," it invites trouble. Sometimes polite speech can be so overdone as to be sarcastic and offensive.

CHAPTER 7

MEETINGS: AGREEMENT IS THE OBJECTIVE

Try to Enliven Meetings—But Don't Lose Control

☛ Understand the aims of the meeting before speaking. Don't take on the role of the one who stirs things up unless asked.

☛ After grasping the flow of the meeting, become the mood maker. Good meeting skills can expand your human network.

☛ Watch your language. If your speech is either too polite or too familiar it can put a damper on the meeting.

☛ Avoid these three: 1. emotional utterances; 2. excessive circumlocution; 3. argumentiveness or stubbornness.

☛ If you want to make the meeting a success, start with the seating arrangements. Those who like to talk should be kept apart from each other.

☛ Plan to answer questions and counter any complaints that are likely to come up. Have an alternative plan and other materials ready when needed.

☛ To be truly prepared for the meeting, don't neglect your nemawashi, the advance informal discussions of the meeting topic.

☛ It's not good manners to criticize a meeting after it's over.

A Meeting's Success or Failure Depends on the One Who Moves It Ahead

"Learn from my failure," says Mr. T, a four-year employee who was chosen to run his first meeting: "I double-checked all the arrangements: the time, the room reservation, everything. After preparing all the materials and distributing them to all present, I was looking forward to a perfect meeting. But the meeting ended without deciding anything, and I was scolded by the attendees as well as by my boss. When I had a chance to think about it later, I realized it was because it wasn't clear in my mind what the objectives of the meeting were."

All meetings have a specific purpose. If the point of the meeting is to solve a problem, you have to begin by analyzing the problem. If the aim is to develop ideas, then you use brainstorming and other techniques to coax ideas from those attending. In short, how the meeting proceeds depends on what the purpose of the meeting is.

Selecting the Attendees

The selection of those invited to attend the meeting is one important element in the process. Keep the following points in mind as you work on selecting people:

☛ You must balance the ranks of the main attendees.

☛ Do the attendees feel there is a problem related to the main topic? Are they in a position to give a responsible opinion on the subject?

☛ Are they from the departments related to or affected by the main topic? Do they have the authority to plan and implement the main items on the agenda for the meeting?

After considering these points, you have taken your first step toward having a fruitful meeting.

Be Careful about Seating

We all have our own individual personality traits. When it comes to meetings, there are those who become high-spirited and active and those who will only listen to what others are saying without volunteering anything themselves, including a few who will doze off during the meeting. As a result, it's necessary to take some care in how you seat everyone.

☛ Do not seat those who will have a lot to say in positions next to each other: A and B, H and I, etc. And, more importantly, don't line them up alongside the meeting chairman because differences between them will develop, the discussion will become rancorous and others won't have the opportunity to speak.

☛ Those who don't plan to say very much will naturally gravitate towards seats that are away from the meeting chairman. Assign positions A and I for them as this will make it easy for others to speak and facilitate the exchange of opinions.

☛ People from the same department or section will naturally want to take up positions next to each other. Since meetings are not the occasion for different departments to open hostilities with each other, give adequate consideration to distributing members of the same department so as to permit greater interaction between everyone at the meeting.

☛ The opponents of the proposal will tend to sit together at the lower end of the table facing the chair. If in advance you position one of the proposal's advocates in one of those seats, the flow of the discussion can be changed.

To make sure everyone adheres to the chairman's plan for the seating arrangements, make place cards in advance and have them in place before the attendees arrive.

Your Real Ability Will Stand Out at Meetings

Become the Mood Maker

Whether it's a party or any other type of gathering, a mood maker is always necessary. So it should surprise no one that this is true also for business meetings. People always notice the one who leads the others into discussions and can end a meeting on an upbeat note.

Sample Seating Arrangement

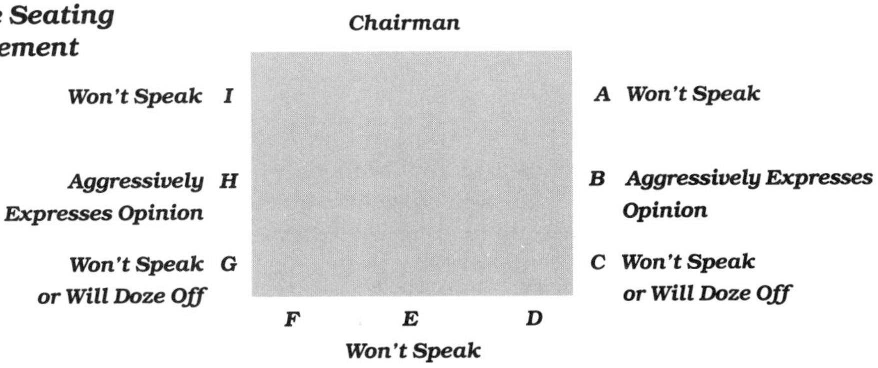

Ten Ironclad Rules for Meetings

1. Begin and end on time.

2. Holding a meeting for no compelling reason is an evasion of your responsibility as a manager. Call a meeting only after carefully considering whether it's necessary or not.

3. Don't sit in for someone else at a meeting and don't send anyone to sit in for you. Let people know about upcoming meetings and distribute materials to them well ahead of the appointed time.

4. Summarize materials. It's best if you can get all the main points on a single piece of paper.

Know Your Role

If you ask someone who is experienced in chairing meetings, you'll find that there are times when you have to assign roles in advance to assure that the meeting proceeds smoothly. This means, for example, asking one of the participants before the meeting to express a certain idea or take a specific position when you call on him to speak later.

Since people who are well informed about the issues will often be chosen to chair the meeting, adequate advance preparation is indispensable.

Learn to Use Pauses

If you are ever confronted with a completely unexpected question at a business meeting, don't get flustered. Give yourself a minute to organize your thoughts before answering by playing for time. Try asking the person to rephrase the question or ask the others present whether they understood or have their own question about what was asked. By coming back with a question at such a point you will gain the time you need to fashion your own response.

Never Engage in an Emotional Counterargument

As people begin to argue their opinions more forcefully and the arguments grow hotter, the tendency is to defend one's position tenaciously more out of a desire to save face than for any other reason. At such times, it's important to be able to coolly and objectively listen to others' opinions no matter how unreasonable you think they are. A meeting is no place to start a fight.

Aim for Concise Expression

At meetings, those who don't speak to the point end up irritating the others. The best approach is to make an outline of what you want to say in your mind before speaking, and then when your turn comes, say it within three minutes at most. The following methods can be helpful:

1. Bulleted Method: "I am now going to introduce three opinions. The first is. . ."

2. Conclusion Up Front: Tell the meeting what it is you believe and then tell them why.

3. Deductive Reasoning: "This is my conclusion. I have based this conclusion on the following principles."

4. Inductive Reasoning: "Please consider these five items of data first. What we can conclude based on this data is. . ."

Taking Notes at Meetings

A middle-level manager at an insurance company, Mr. F, always stands out at meetings. Here he tells how he uses note-taking to his advantage: "Whatever is said at a meeting that strikes me as really true or, on the contrary, as very doubtful, I jot down on a pad of paper. Then when it's time to ask questions, I refer to my notes. Whatever you find worthy of recording from another speaker's remarks in this way constitutes the key points of the speech. Of course, even opinions that strike an emotional chord in you still have to be treated in the same businesslike manner."

Excuses Won't Work

When you begin your remarks by taking a humble approach and saying you are not a good speaker or you're not used to speaking before a group, you're really only trying to make excuses for yourself. Say what you have to say with self-confidence and you'll be a lot more persuasive.

No Post-Meeting Quarterbacking

During the meeting, they're eager to agree, but once the meeting is over they find fault with everything. "What he said is crazy… that guy doesn't understand anything…" The complaints are endless.

If you have an opinion at a meeting, you should have the courage to express it at the meeting, not afterward.

Be Careful of the Five Meeting-Busters

Outsiders: Those who come late or get up and leave their seats, creating an unpleasant atmosphere. They make absurd statements.

Replayers: When you finally think you've reached a decision and are ready to breathe a sigh of relief, you can count on these people to say something that will start everyone steaming again.

Destroyers: Quick to catch any slip of the tongue, these meeting wreckers attack especially when they see progress being made.

Invaders: They come up with issues that are completely unrelated to the topic at hand. Just when you have everyone at the meeting stirred up over an issue, they're sure to ask a question that's clearly off the mark.

Silencers: Why don't they say something? Is it because they think silence makes them look better, or because to speak would be undignified? Or is it because they just don't understand anything that's going on at the meeting?

5. Keep down the number of those who need to attend the meeting, and don't invite certain people out of a sense of loyalty. A good rule to keep in mind is that the limit for a discussion is 12 people.

6. A meeting that ends without a conclusion is nothing but a glorified tea party. Cover every item on the agenda fully.

7. A meeting that lasts an hour is best. One that runs two hours is acceptable. One that lasts three hours or more is counterproductive.

8. Don't monopolize the discussion. If each person limits his or her remarks to within three minutes, everyone can be heard.

9. Announce the points which have been decided and put them into action quickly.

10. Always consider whether the meeting has been cost effective.

CHAPTER 8

BUSINESS WRITING THAT COMMUNICATES WARMTH

Word-Processed or Handwritten?

- ☛ Even a single handwritten stroke on business correspondence makes a difference.
- ☛ Send faxes to busy people.
- ☛ In word processing, you have a free hand with the layout and size of the typeface. But the first consideration should be readability.
- ☛ Letters of thanks, get-well wishes, letters to the bereaved and apologies should be handwritten to show your sincerity.
- ☛ Always use letters to express thanks. A written note is more effective than a telephone call.
- ☛ People who are good at writing letters are good with people. Use letters as a tool to build your human network.

Faxes and Word-Processed Documents Can Communicate Warmth

"Our office was completely inundated with water from a typhoon," recalls trading company general affairs manager Mr. A. "But in the middle of all this mess, the first message we got from the outside world came through our fax machine. I was so happy I could have cried."

When you're really busy it's often irritating to get phone calls. For communicating with busy people, faxes are the right answer, and they are all the more sincere when they're handwritten. Considering the time and the place is the essential step in becoming good at correspondence. Master the use of fax, word processing and handwritten notes and choose the appropriate means of communication for each occasion.

1

Word Processing + a Handwritten Touch

Always add a handwritten touch to routine word-processed documents and letters. You can reach the other person's heart by writing a brief note like "Hope you can help with this," or "With your cooperation, we won't have anything to worry about."

Even for letters of rejection or complaint, it's advisable to add a line that shows your consideration for the other person. By saying that you understand that there must be extenuating circumstances or that the other person must be extremely busy, you make the tone of the letter softer and make it easier for him to understand and accept your point.

☛ In important places, it's wise to increase the size of characters and underline them. Use smaller characters when referring to yourself or your company. You'll want to use the various capabilities of word processing to the fullest to create documents that are easy to read and show the greatest respect to the other person.

☛ When using a word processor to write a personal message, print it out on personal or colored stationery to avoid giving the impression of a formal or official document.

☛ Check word-processed documents carefully for typos and misspellings before sending them. Small mistakes can make you the butt of jokes and may damage the credibility of your company in the eyes of your customers.

Use Faxes Skillfully for Greater Effectiveness

Mr. Y, a mid-level manager at a major publishing house in Tokyo tells how his office pursues efficiency: "We are now faxing all messages and other communications to the people we know are busiest. That way, when they get the chance to deal with the matter, they'll have all the information right in front of them." Instead of continuing to call and leave messages for someone who's out of the office, communication is a lot more certain when you send a note by facsimile. You also don't run the risk of having a receptionist or other third party make a mistake in taking down the message.

☛ Use clear instructions for the handling of fax transmissions.

☛ If you plan to send a very long document that will tie up the other person's fax machine for quite a while, get his or her permission before you start sending. In such cases, it's sometimes more considerate to have the documents delivered by hand.

Handwriting Expresses Your Sincerity

In an age when word-processed documents are everywhere, handwritten notes have acquired a special cachet of their own. Word-processed thank-you notes, get-well wishes and letters of regret look too routine and unfeeling. Handwritten notes express your sincerity better.

Rules to Live by

☛ Never forget to show respect for the other person in writing.

☛ When writing the other person's name or title, don't ever let it run onto the next line. If there isn't enough room on one line to write it completely, start on the next line.

☛ Be careful not to mix in your own opinion or ideas in official correspondence. When you write for the company it is to express the company's desires. When in doubt, ask your boss to review and approve your correspondence.

Using Letters to Build Your Network: Become an Active Letter Writer!

Writing letters is extremely effective in building a network of contacts in the business world. Reading a handwritten note, the person can see your face and remember your personality in each stroke of the pen. And, unlike a phone call, the letter can remain in the hands of the receiver.

An additional important point that shouldn't be overlooked is that the recipient of the letter will probably read it when he has more time in a relaxed atmosphere, conditions that favor a deepening of the feeling of closeness. This is why people who are active letter writers also have large human networks.

Using the Unexpected Letter to Your Advantage

"Everyone sends year-end greeting cards to friends or other people who have favored them in the past," explains Mr. K, an executive in the office of the president of a large office automation equipment manufacturer. "But in that season, I like to send printed cards thanking those who have helped me over the past months. Of course, I don't forget to send new year's cards as well."

Send Picture Post Cards on Trips

"The best picture post cards," says architect Mr. G, "are those that show breathtakingly beautiful scenes." Post cards are just the right tool to stay in touch with those in your network with whom you may not have spoken recently.

CHAPTER 9

TRAINING OUTSIDE THE COMPANY

Make Everyone Your Teacher—You Just Have to Have the Right Antenna to Catch Their Signals

☛ A surprising number of great inventions have been discovered by people who come up with ideas when they're not at work. You can learn a lot simply by avoiding the same old work routine and going to different places to socialize with different people.

Educating Yourself in Visits to Companies

"Whenever we do business for the first time with a new company," explains Mr. G, a manager at a well-known heavy electric manufacturer, "we have them show us not only their offices but also their plant sites. This is necessary for both sides to get really serious about each other.

"I usually plan to stay overnight on trips to the factory," he continues. "And when I go drinking with factory personnel, they tell me all about concepts or production management know-how that I'd never even dreamt about before." Mr. G's method of using simple visits to other companies for his own purposes has proven very effective for him.

Discovery Through Contact with Different Types of Work

You link your company to a related one by computer. Two companies send people to study outside the company when they set up a joint venture. Or you simply organize a study group together. No matter what it is, whenever you get the chance to learn from other companies, take it. There was once a time when people said the three skills a businessman needed to get along with people were karaoke, mah-jongg and golf, but that time is long gone. The new era calls for study, building a network of business and other contacts and constant self-improvement.

To Succeed, Study Groups Need Realistic Objectives

Study groups that are set up to blindly follow trends don't last long. To succeed, the group needs one or more of the following elements:

☛ Each member has his or her own strength, and learning takes place through an exchange of information. There are many examples of such salon-like circles.

☛ A group can also have a strong leader or specialist who draws a circle of people to study around him or her.

☛ The group divides responsibilities for studying a topic, surveys and researches it, then works to improve the understanding of each of its members.

Study groups take all sorts of forms, but to be fruitful, all of the members must have a clear idea of the group's objectives and must be dedicated enough to find the time to attend meetings faithfully.

You should also give some thought to creating the proper atmosphere within the group. Because all participants are business warriors, you have to be prepared for those times when members will carry on fierce information wars with each other. On the other hand, you should keep in mind that without such tension the group will lose its vigor and die. In effect, the basic rule is that group members can attack each other as aggressively as they wish to the extent that it does not interfere with the balance of harmony that permits the smooth operation of the group.

Using Your Studies

Wherever you turn you can see study groups flourishing. By participating actively, you can earn some return no matter how small. Inaction in the group, however, means you'll never see a return on the money, or time you invested in your studies.

☛ Participate even in those groups in which study is most difficult.

☛ Prepare to take notes.

☛ Your instructor is an expert in his field. By not asking him questions, you are permitting a valuable opportunity to slip away.

☛ If you don't at least exchange cards with the people sitting next to you, you have wasted your time.

☛ If you take what you have learned in your study group and assemble your coworkers to report on it to them, you'll find that it will be a lot clearer in your own mind. By putting it into simple memo form, it will become even clearer.

☛ The temporary satisfaction you get after studying something is meaningless unless you apply it. You have to take the know-how you acquire and use it to achieve results in your job. If you don't, you'll soon forget it.

Be Willing to Try Anything

Publishing company manager Mr. K talks about how he started using a computer: "In the beginning the idea of using a word processor in my job intrigued me, so I started doing drafts on floppy disks. Now I realize how much time and energy it has saved. And I only started doing it because it seemed like fun."

Today, it's extremely important to anticipate the fundamental skills and technologies you'll need for the coming era and acquire them without wasting time. It's often the case that you or your company alone may not be able to master these valuable capabilities. When that's the situation, you'll want to take advantage of opportunities to participate and build contacts among managers from other fields.

You can also work to deepen the relationship of trust and interdependence you have with companies you do business with and learn through this avenue as well.

Manners for Study Groups

☛ It's bad manners to attend a group meeting and just listen. Don't just sit on the sidelines watching. Always prepare information that will be of interest to others at the meeting and be ready to present it.

☛ Don't take up everyone's time by asking questions that benefit no one else but yourself, or asking for advice with problems that you alone are dealing with on your job.

☛ Don't ask another member who is already very busy to help you with research or to arrange an introduction for you.

☛ Don't introduce office hierarchical relationships into the study group. All members of the group are to be treated as equals and as individuals.

CHAPTER 10

COLLECTING INFORMATION

Give and Take is the Way to Go

☛ The information you have at your command is directly proportional to the number of your business friends and acquaintances. Cultivate your network.

☛ When there's information someone needs to get from you, provide it freely.

☛ Become friendly with others on the intellectual level. That's the best way to get information from people.

☛ Keep an open mind so you'll always be able to take advantage of fresh information.

☛ Details are what count in "human" information.

☛ Never read highly confidential corporate materials on the train as you commute to and from work.

☛ You'll find the keys to understanding a company buried in its public relations materials and employee communications publications.

To Get, You Have to Give Data as Well

With office automation equipment undergoing one change after another, it's sometimes difficult to decide which products to buy. Mr. N, a manager at a stone material supplier, tells this story: "I was looking at a particular computer model, when the salesman told me that if I waited three months there would soon be a brand new model with many more functions. This was very valuable information for me and I returned the favor by letting him know that we were planning to introduce this sort of computer into our subsidiary companies as well."

The salesman could have just made the sale, but he decided to put himself in the customer's shoes and offered some useful information. And for doing so he received some valuable information in return. Information flow requires give and take. Give information freely and you'll get a lot more back.

With a Little Intellectual Curiosity, You Can Become an Information Source, Too

A good information exchange begins with the confidence you create by giving useful, correct information to the other person even though it does not benefit you. You can start by keeping an eye out for items that might interest some other person as you go through your own daily information collection activities. If there's a memo that might be useful to that person, make a copy of it and write a little note on it to ask if he is aware of it. Then send it to him by facsimile.

If you think that you'll be able to collect new information at parties attended by many people in your industry, you are making a big mistake. You won't get anything if you just plan to listen to what others say. Use intellectual conversation as a tool to arouse the curiosity of the other person and start communicating. Depending on how interesting the conversation is, you can then get an active exchange going.

React with Sensitivity

Mr. N. also tells what happens when information that's offered goes unused: "More times than I'd like to remember I'll give someone very useful information and then not hear anything else about it. When that happens, I usually worry that perhaps the information was meaningless and of no use. At the same time, I make a mental note not to provide the person with information again."

When someone gives you new information, no matter how trivial it seems, be sure to report it so that your organization can take advantage. Information takes on real value when it is used properly.

"Someone told me that a key person in one of our client companies had been promoted," explains Mr. N. "When I met him, I was able to congratulate him on his new job. Right then and there he told me that he'd continue to order from us in his new position. That should be enough to demonstrate how reporting in detail can pay off for your organization."

You can also make ample use of seemingly minor matters. People who create new concepts and plans are always in search of information. They're able to sort through a mass of data and pull out exactly what they need. You can become as skilled as they are in both uncovering the right information and transmitting it accurately to those who need it.

Business Otsukiai Depends on Good Information

Unleakable Information

☛ In a moment of carelessness, information that's supposed to stay inside the company is sometimes leaked to outsiders. Always have what you can and can't speak about clear in your mind. No matter how much others call for give-and-take, if you talk about everything going on inside the company, the information you reveal will lose its value.

To Get Information on Related Companies

☛ Everyday, go through all major newspapers that cover business, trade newspapers and magazines. If you find an item of interest, like a shift in top executives of a related company, clip it and put it in your files.

☛ Obtain copies of the company's employee and external communications publications.

☛ Become close to the secretaries of the top executives. They'll answer all your questions and let you know about upcoming changes of top executives.

☛ Whenever there is a reshuffling of management, documents detailing the changes are sent to the appropriate departments. Collect and digest these documents and you'll be able to draw up a complete map of the personnel in the company.

☛ Details related to new products are regarded as extremely confidential by companies. Talking about the name of a new product or other details in a commuter train or other public places is strictly forbidden. Worse yet is taking out documents related to new products and reviewing them in public places. In many cases, information is collected from strange sources and makes its way to rival companies.

☛ Other types of information you should keep secret are:

- Upcoming personnel changes
- Technical and other tie-ups
- Issues before the board of directors
- Feuding inside the company

Keep Confidential Files

File 1: There are many people who write the date of the meeting and other details on business cards they receive, but it's even more valuable if you add that person's interests, such as fishing, golf, stamps, karaoke singing, etc. Once you've indexed these for your files, you can start compiling a list of people and telephone numbers to consult on any number of topics.

File 2: After entertaining someone who you're doing business with, always jot down a few notes about him that same day. Record what songs he sang, the type of liquor he preferred, golf handicap, place of birth, schools and universities attended, marital status and children and other such data. Getting this type of information would normally involve a lot of legwork, but you'll be able to collect this—and more—easily and naturally as you entertain.

PART 2

OTSUKIAI INSIDE THE COMPANY

CHAPTER 1

FELLOW EMPLOYEES

Partners, Not Pals

☛ It's natural to be friends with those in your section or department. But go a step further and make friends throughout your organization.

☛ Your best friend in the company, the person everyone respects for his brainpower and your "mentor" can all be assets. Cultivate these three people properly.

☛ Remember that you get part of your salary for working with people with whom you don't necessarily get along.

☛ Cheerful greetings for your fellow employees make work go smoothly.

☛ The "Worst Three" topics for conversation are: where one lives, promotions and factions within the company.

☛ Gossip and spreading rumors can ruin people's careers. Don't start or spread tales.

☛ Don't ever give the appearance of immorality to anyone.

Creating Lively and Stimulating Workplace Relationships

Mr. K works for a large food processing company. Here is his account of an employee who was lost because of the absence of a lively working atmosphere: "I was awfully disappointed to lose such a talented systems engineer. After arranging for him to have his own private office and creating an environment for him to do things the way he thought best, I thought to myself, 'Now for sure he won't have any cause for dissatisfaction with this job.'"

Unfortunately, the employee in question left the company where he had been working closely only with his genial 60-year old boss, Mr. K, to join a data processing company where there were more people from his own generation.

When one is asked what is more important, the content of the job or the place where the job is done, it's only natural to say it's the content of the job. But if the truth be told, it's the workplace itself. People are controlled and motivated by emotional input from diverse human relationships. There are more than a few people who have quit jobs, complaining that they could no longer stand the particular relationships in their former companies. Making the workplace a good place in which to live is an essential job for every man and woman in business.

Learning about Other Employees

Mr. T, a manager at an executive search firm, explains what his experience has taught him about interpersonal relationships on the job:

"Over the years, I've found that when someone won't do what he or she has been asked to do, it usually is because the one who has asked just doesn't understand that person well enough. For that reason, I have made three rules that I want my people to follow:

☛ Be a shrewd judge of those around you, know their potential.

☛ Work on becoming friendly with them. Establish solid ties.

☛ Motivate them.

"Of these rules, the most important, of course, is the first. Once you truly know the other person, you can use that as a basis for mastering the other two."

Maintain a Proper Distance

"Your wife's sick? Then, why don't you go home early today. I'll take care of your word-processing work," a colleague offers. As a result, an insignificant typo he makes changes the meaning of your report and results in a failure for you and your section.

It's up to you to do your own job. All employees have to maintain this posture, as tough and unbending as it seems. Each person knows the minor details of his or her job and the current status of the work flow, and no one else can step in and do it as well. For this reason, you must always maintain strict separation between your job and your feelings for other employees. To maintain an appropriate distance, the proper attitude is critical.

☛ When another employee confides in you or talks about what is troubling him or her, you can listen, but never inquire or pry into another's personal affairs.

☛ Sharing rumors or gossip about other people with your friends makes you feel closer to them, but that closeness is only superficial. On the other hand, the damage you can do to others' reputations can be very large and lasting.

☛ Praising someone can be taken by others in the office as somehow slighting to them. Before you praise anyone, think about the consequences carefully.

☛ You lose the proper distance when you speak as if you control the person, when you speak harshly to someone or when you flatter someone.

☛ When you become emotional or upset about something someone else has said or done, don't talk about it. If you're still troubled about whether you ought to say something to someone, think it over at leisure, and find a better way to say it.

☛ No matter how close you are to your mah-jongg or fishing pals from the office, you can not carry that attitude over into your daily work life. Maintain the same posture to everyone in the company.

Little Things that Make for a Cheery Workplace

Here's a list of do's and don't's to help you keep the office a pleasant and bright place in which to work:

☛ Schedule vacation and other time off so that it interferes as little as possible with work.

☛ After taking a day off from work, be sure to say a word or two to apologize for any inconvenience it caused to those who work with you.

☛ Don't shirk any of the chores you have been assigned.

☛ When asked a question, respond clearly. Saying nothing creates problems.

☛ Don't break in on meetings or carry on a loud conversation next to someone speaking on the phone. Both mean disrupting the company's work.

☛ Don't borrow money from or lend it to other employees. If someone else pays your share of a bill, settle the debt immediately.

☛ When borrowing something in the office, it's best to apologize for the inconvenience. Don't get in the bad habit of borrowing other people's desks or sitting in their chairs.

☛ Don't ask others to run personal errands. However, if someone is going to the post office, for example, and asks if anyone needs anything there, you can take advantage of the opportunity.

☛ When you travel on business, bring back souvenirs. It brightens up the office atmosphere.

☛ Be cheerful when greeting or showing appreciation to your fellow employees.

CHAPTER 2

GETTING ALONG WITH YOUR BOSS

The Accent is on Softness

☛ If you know your boss's personality, you can become a bulwark against friction and confrontations with other people.

☛ Report. Contact. Consult.

☛ Observe the chain of command. Managers should scrutinize reports before sending them back to the senior manager. Show what you're made of by making sure they check them.

☛ You're not supposed to be a yes-man. If you're really doing your job right, there'll be times when you'll have to say no.

☛ Your boss also has a boss. Learn to look for the deeper significance of his directions.

☛ Put yourself in your boss's place when thinking about the job. If you do, you'll be able to grasp what your role is.

To Eliminate Doubt and Stiff Relations, Be Ready to Strike First

There are many business people who think that there would be nothing to equal the pleasure of choosing your own boss. But since it's not your fate to select your boss, it would be more productive to put your heart into learning how to work under any boss and do a good job rather than just complaining.

Categories of Bosses

Some bosses say they like subordinates who work quietly and obediently. Others say they prefer those who can be left to their own resources and score by themselves now and then.

Mr. K, who worked under 12 bosses at a major advertising agency in Tokyo, offers these thoughts on the different types of bosses he has known and how to deal with them:

☛ One boss was eager to argue any point with you, but could never seem to make an accurate evaluation of a situation. Because he lacked management skills, he was sent for additional training to qualify him for his position. After that, he recognized my abilities.

☛ Another boss used himself as the standard by which he judged his subordinates. I'll always remember the time he finally recognized my abilities. "I see," he said, "so you can get work done that way too? You really have some good ideas."

☛ Another is the type that sees one good part of something and then assumes the whole thing is good. I worked hard to win him over by always dressing sharply, keeping the files on my desk neat and orderly and watching the details to which he paid the most attention.

☛ Then there was the boss whose mind was so sharp that he was well beyond my powers to size up. They say that if you look at a razor under a microscope you can see that the blade is pitted and bent in places and not as sharp as it looks to the naked eye. So instead of work topics, I talked with him about his dreams and literature, and gradually got to know him.

Mr. K adds a few cautions: "When you go about this process of sizing up and getting to know your boss, the worst thing you can do is be obvious about it. You should make your approach gradually and subtly as you become a better observer of his behavior. Keep in mind that this process will make your work go more smoothly, too. And, of course, remember that sycophancy and flattery will most likely get you nowhere."

Report. Contact. Consult.

When You've Been Told to Do a Job

☛ If it's a difficult job, ask about any points that you're not clear on and how the work is to proceed. Then, as quickly as possible, dig up the information requested by your boss plus some additional details you think might be helpful. Remember that your boss is very busy. Avoid having to go back to disturb him by asking details about the request later.

☛ Pay attention to answering phone calls for your boss and to dealing with your boss's superior. You can learn how your section's work is regarded in the company and its importance.

Hints to Help Get Along with a Tough Boss

• Even though you think he's tough, make opportunities to get to know him better.

• Praise your boss to a third person.

• If your boss shows antagonism to you, pretend you don't notice it.

• If he tries to involve you in a confrontation, feign ignorance.

• If you have to find fault with one of his proposals or other ideas, don't become involved in an emotional exchange. Stick to the issues, and cover all of the points in question.

☛ When your work starts to pile up and there's a chance you won't finish a job by the deadline, explain the situation to your boss and consult with him on changing the work flow. Once you make an order of priority for completing tasks and arrange work assignments accordingly, your life will become a lot easier.

When There Are Doubts about the Progress of the Job

☛ Report immediately and find out what your boss thinks. Do your best to present the current status of the job in a brief and easy-to-understand format. When documents or cooperation from other departments are needed, report to your boss and secure his understanding before proceeding.

☛ When the work begins to take a new direction, and you are confused about making the right decision, you need to know what your boss thinks. Consult him.

When the Report is Ready

☛ It's nearly impossible to turn in a perfect exam in the business world. But two or three days before you have to turn in a report, it's advisable to ask others to help improve its accuracy. In those two or three days, you can bring your grade up 40 points or so. Who knows, with the right help, your report may get that elusive perfect grade.

Bosses Are Always Hard to Handle

There are times when all you can do is change the tone of your voice and try to cope.

"You can't just be a yes-man," says telephone company executive Mr. H. "When you think your boss is going to make the wrong decision on some matter, have the self-confidence to tell him so. That's your job as his subordinate."

Here's a summary of what Mr. H has observed in his years in management.

What Are You Getting at?

Even though you have taken pains to explain a situation, your boss is irritated and isn't listening. So change your approach and try again. A sloppy, time-consuming explanation will make your boss antagonistic because he must routinely battle for time. Start by presenting the conclusion clearly, and then concisely show the process you used to arrive at it. Only go into details when you need to in order to answer questions. You should also reflect on whether some of the irritation your boss showed was in reaction to what he took to be your servile attitude.

I Don't Want to Hear Any Excuses

When your boss barks at you that he doesn't want to hear any excuses even though you're only trying to explain what happened, it's enough to make you lose track of what you are trying to convey. At such a point, the only acceptable response is to apologize and continue with the bare outlines of the explanation. Later, when you have a chance, go over what you said to see if anything in your explanation could possibly be taken as mere excuse making. After being treated like this, it's best to lower your profile and allow for a cooling-off period.

When You Don't Agree and Have to Rebut

No boss likes to have his ideas bluntly knocked down by subordinates, so when you have to rebut a boss's ideas, try to stay as calm as possible. For bosses who have a particular dislike for others criticizing their ideas, wait until the problem area comes up in the discussion. Before expressing your disagreement, preface your remarks by telling the superior that you yourself hadn't noticed the problem until now.

When Offering Advice on a Plan or Idea

When your boss is relaxed and calm, try to match his mood if you have to consult with him. Pushing ideas too hard and with too much familiarity and confidence can only earn his antagonism. For a boss who tends to avoid responsibility, it's sometimes productive to take one of his colleagues along when you consult with him. There are sometimes cases when, because of his position, a boss can not give you the go-ahead for a project. Find out what the reason is and then work out a new approach that takes that reason into account.

I'll Leave It in Your Hands

When you have a good relationship with your boss, you can take him at his word, but make detailed reports anyway to be safe.

Sudden Reprimands

Before you start to sulk about a boss who gets angry over nothing at all and is unacceptably moody, try to understand how someone can blow up when he constantly sees things that leave him dissatisfied. There are also bosses who reprimand those to whom they intend to entrust important work. In any case, be on your toes and listen carefully to what your boss tells you.

- ***Socialize with someone who is close to your boss, and then become friendly with your boss himself through this person.***

- ***Show interest in his hobbies or his area of experitse. You can improve the relationship by getting him to teach you about these areas.***

- ***Assist your boss with his work in some way that's not obvious. This will be passed along to him by someone else later.***

- ***If you can socialize with him under different circumstances than those in the office, you'll be amazed to find how much you have in common.***

To Help Maintain a Good Working Relationship with Your Boss

Provide Information Freely

Report raw data, including newspaper and magazine clippings and other information freely and promptly to your boss. When he's busy, jot the information down and leave it on his desk.

Don't Indulge in Gossip

The senior manager of another section whom your manager trusts has been spreading gossip about him. Out of personal loyalty to your manager you want to tell him what's going on, but you have to avoid that impulse. Human relationships are nothing if not complicated. You never know when two people will become alienated from each other or if and when they'll ever make up again. When it comes to such relationships in the office, silence is golden.

When Showing Appreciation, Consider the Person's Status

It's meaningless when you tell a big-shot senior manager in the directors' office that he did a wonderful job. But if his fellow senior executives were to tell him the same thing, he would be so happy that he would almost be moved to tears.

Observe the Chain of Command in Circulating Reports

Don't assume that a report written by a senior manager should be sent back to him just because the manager to whom it was to be circulated for review is not in the office. Doing this means you are ignoring the manager's responsibility to run a final check on the report. If you don't respect people's posts and responsibilities, your colleagues will shun you.

Always Have a Strategy

When your work stalls at your immediate superior's desk, schedule a meeting to discuss the task and have your boss's boss attend it. In this way, you can get the job done without causing your boss to lose face. In fact, if you handle it skillfully enough, your boss may even thank you for it. But work out your strategy carefully in advance to avoid giving the impression you're going over your boss's head.

There Are Times When You Must Keep Your Lips Sealed

When your boss asks your opinion of one of his colleagues, mix seven parts praise with three parts truth, even if it's someone you find unbearable. Likewise, when your boss angrily demands that you tell him who has been speaking ill of him, keep your lips sealed. That sort of thing is for him to find out himself.

When the Boss Takes the Credit, Don't Flinch

There are some bosses who talk as if a proposal that was actually suggested and worked on by one of their subordinates was really their own creation. If this happens to you, don't show your anger by sulking.

Fuel company executive Mr. O offers this advice: "It's the subordinate's job to educate and cultivate the boss. I, for one, give my boss the data and materials he needs to do the job and have him make the proposal. If the proposal carries the boss's name, it usually gets a lot further than it would with my name on it."

Called on the Carpet? Say "Thank You"

When you're harshly scolded by your boss for a mistake you've made, let him know that you are grateful for it. Here's a good way to put it: "I'm very sorry about the mistake I made. With your help and guidance I'm sure it won't happen again." When you are scolded but you don't know why, it's best to wait a day or so before you go back to dealing with him the way you did before the reprimand. Once the boss's psychological burden is eased a bit, he'll calm down also.

Outside the Company

Mr. Y, an executive in charge of product development for a large consumer electronics manufacturer, has this advice about socializing with the boss: "Whenever the work really gets hard, my boss always wants to do something to make it up to me, for example, by inviting me out to drink or have dinner. No matter what job I have to put down to do it, I always go with him."

For after-hours socializing, the general rule should be not to cause the other person, boss or subordinate, any inconvenience.

☛ Even if he is the boss, don't let him pay the check. Split the bill.

☛ Never drink so much that it interferes with your work the following day. Don't go to "second parties" after the first event ends. Drinking so much that someone else has to take care of you is inexcusable.

☛ Don't gossip about the company.

☛ If you're invited to someone's house, you should go, but be sure not to dress too informally. If you're at a loss for how to dress, a suit and tie are always proper attire. Be polite and don't overstay.

CHAPTER 3

BRINGING UP YOUR SUBORDINATES

Catch Up to Me and Then Pass Me

☛ Your attitude should be, "stick to me during working hours, but after five, you're on your own."

☛ As your subordinates grow, business grows with them. Give them as many chances as possible to develop.

☛ When subordinates come up with ideas or advice, hear them out.

☛ You'll never be trusted unless you can keep things to yourself.

☛ When you praise someone, be specific about what merits the praise.

☛ Distinguish between emotions and the needs of the job. When the boss reprimands someone, it should be for a reason that everyone in the office understands.

☛ Keep your subordinates' spirits up, and every so often spend a little of your own money on them.

Each One of You Adds to Our Fighting Power

"What your section accomplishes is really nothing more than what your subordinates are able to achieve," advises Mr. G, a senior manager from the marketing department of a large gas utility. "In bringing my subordinates along, I always try to foster in them the spirit that if they attempt something, they'll be able to do it. For example, it's really important for their confidence to make that first sale. So before they set out, I'll go through their area without telling anyone, and do some preliminary sales work to make it easier for them to be successful."

As Mr. G's story indicates, training subordinates is no small part of a manager's job. Continuously turning out people who can do the best job in the least amount of time with the smallest amount of labor improves the performance of the section and the department, and is a factor in winning promotions. But wholehearted devotion to efficiency does not allow for proper cultivation of your subordinates' talents. People can also work for the sake of efficiency, but they are naturally motivated by a desire for satisfaction.

Turning Depression into Drive

Rejecting Plans

Someone has created what appears to be the ideal plan, but you decide that, while it looks fine on paper, it won't get enough support within the company at this point. "It's just a little too premature," you explain as you reject it. But the subordinate is so depressed about things after hearing this, he can't bring himself to get back to work. At such a point, rather than getting angry at the person, it's wiser to start talking. Explain things, giving examples taken from a broader perspective, and show him the parts of the plan that were found to be the weak points. As you slowly make the person understand your thinking, you will also be able to move his or her training along that much further.

After Reprimanding for A Failure

☛ For the sensitive types, it's best to quickly find some task he or she can handle and then order them to do it. After being reprimanded, they will tend to worry that you have lost confidence in them, so this is just what they need to cheer them up again.

☛ For those who may show rebellion by taking time off unnecessarily, it's best to ignore such absences and allow for a cooling off period. When they become frustrated and angry at only having busywork to do, give them a task, explaining that it's the sort of work they could do well. Those who rebel do so because of a strong sense of pride. By giving them a little recognition you can play on this pride and get them motivated once again.

☛ For the ordinary subordinate, scold as much as necessary and then just forget about it.

Building Confidence

For subordinates who lack the confidence to do more responsible work, it's best to try to get to know them better in different surroundings. Printing company manager Mr. H tells this story of one successful case: "When I took my subordinate along to a computer fair, I found that he was very knowledgeable about computers. He had a computer set up in his home, so I asked him to do analysis of sales data with it. The results were much better than I could have imagined. As a result, we introduced computers into our sales and marketing section and put him in charge. He is now doing more than his part to lift that section's results."

By taking the time to find a special talent his subordinate possessed, and allowing him to expand that talent, Mr. H succeeded in building confidence and broadening the perspective of his young subordinate so that he could do a better job.

To Keep Subordinates Happy, Be Considerate

- ***Don't use subordinates for personal errands.***

- ***It's up to the manager to stop meaningless overtime work — even if it means getting employees to do mountains of work during ordinary business hours.***

- ***Don't just become a messenger boy from top management. Don't lapse into telling employees, "the managing director says such and such." "This is the company's policy" should be the way you approach explaining corporate moves to your subordinates, but be sure you add your own analysis.***

- ***Take the initiative in participating in company-sponsored events and recreation.***

- ***Don't inquire into or express an opinion about the way any employee spends his or her time outside the office.***

Become a Manager for Whom Subordinates Will Make Sacrifices

There exists a natural wall between the manager and the person he manages. To build a relationship of trust that transcends that wall, it's necessary at times to ignore the barrier.

☛ Ask for their help on small matters to show them you're human, too.

☛ When the section has been doing overtime night after night and everyone is completely exhausted, a manager who grumbles loudly, "we can't go on like this," acts as a proxy for the employees in the section and establishes a feeling of closeness with them.

☛ Singing a song to yourself occasionally lets your subordinates see your human side. Performing a series of karate kata or acting in skits can also win smiles of approval.

☛ When you laugh, don't hold back. People notice when you laugh with your mouth but your eyes say something else. People show their humanness when they laugh and when they become angry. Your subordinates will be looking for this in you.

☛ Defend your subordinates even if you have to argue with your superiors. This doesn't do any harm.

☛ If you know someone is interested in a certain subject, every so often buy a book related to that field and give it to them.

Be Easy to Work With

Your section will do its best work if you and your subordinates have a smoothly functioning relationship. Here are several points you should be alert to:

Asking Subordinates to Work on Holidays or Do Overtime

The day before a holiday you ask a subordinate if he's taking off tomorrow. What you're really saying is, "I'll be in tomorrow, how about you?" If the person responds by asking if there's some work to be done and whether he can help, then it's permissible to ask.

If, on the other hand, he says he has an appointment, don't push it. Whatever you do, don't act as if you asked for help and he refused.

Communicating Properly

Explain important policies and other matters fully, using concrete examples when possible. Never appear to be threatening.

When One Person's Work Piles Up

Frequently, the most able subordinate is the one whose work starts to pile up. Often it is the same person who'll try to carry the burden of that work on his shoulders alone, and will ultimately burn out. This is where you, as the boss, have to intervene. Give the subordinate a new employee as an assistant, or have him work with another colleague so that the work can continue smoothly and without interruption. Keep a timetable of your subordinates' work and check it at regular intervals.

Sometimes Everyone Criticizes the Same Person

There are some employees who break the rules so often or have so little discipline that they always attract negative attention. When everyone is fed up with their behavior and about to explode, it's time for the boss to stage a frontal attack and reprimand the person soundly.

When a person realizes how disliked he or she is, the usual response is to try to correct the source of the problem. You can work with people like this and gradually turn them into good employees.

There Are Problem Employees, Too

Complainers

Some employees complain so consistently and loudly that they cast a cloud over the workplace.

The best approach is to see that such people never have the time to complain and gossip with others. Give them lots of assignments to do and get them into the rhythm of working hard.

- ***When you have to speak with an employee on a matter related to advice or consultation, don't do it at your desk. Take ten minutes to spend with the person where you can talk one-on-one.***

- ***When you think it's necessary to talk to someone outside of work, don't walk over to the person's desk where everyone else can hear, and tell him or her that you'd like to talk over coffee. Find a less conspicuous way to create the opportunity, for example, leaving the office together on the way home.***

- ***Don't favor one employee over another. Treat them all equally and make sure that you speak to them all regularly.***

- ***If one of your subordinates is summoned by upper management, be sure to give good suggestions on how to handle oneself in that situation.***

Excessive Borrowers

When employees borrow money and it stays a private matter, there's no reason to say anything. But when loan sharks start calling the office and demanding payment, the office atmosphere becomes poisoned. Meet with the employee and give him a stiff warning. Be careful, however, not to offer to help pay off the loan or become too involved in his affairs. This is merely asking for trouble.

Leaving the Office on Private Matters

When someone spends too much time away from the office for private purposes, a good warning will usually suffice.

When Employees Come to Work Hung Over or Smelling of Alcohol

Warn the person first. If the situation doesn't improve, have someone who is close to that person talk with him about the problem. Another good method is to cut down on his nightlife by sending the person to training classes in the evening.

Psychological Problems

Recommend the person see a specialist and then follow up by finding out the diagnosis. Adjust the quality or amount of the person's work accordingly, and keep a watchful eye on the situation.

Average Monthly Personal Allowance of Salaried Workers (In Yen)

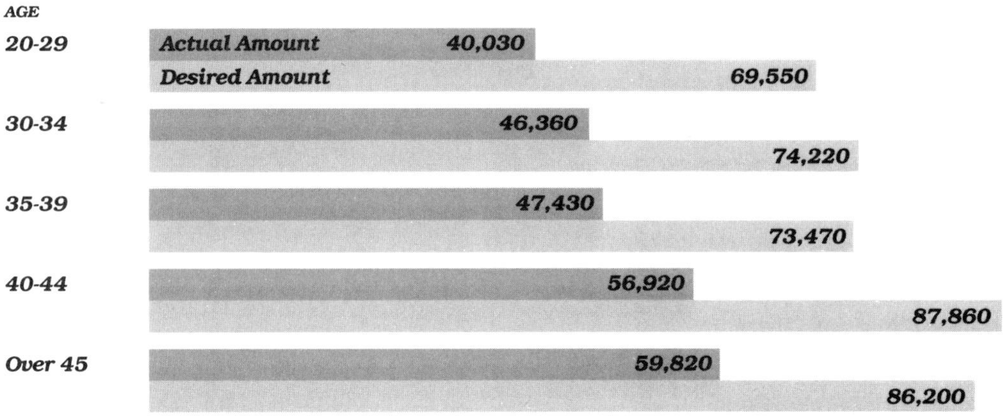

Source: Daihyaku Mutual Life Insurance/1989

CHAPTER 4

CONSIDERATION FOR OTHERS IN THE OFFICE

☛ A thoughtless word from you can make the workplace atmosphere as cold as a deep freezer.

There are All Kinds of People in the Office—Be Flexible

Be Conscious of How You Relate to Women in the Office

Ms. E, a manager at food processing company, recalls her first job: "Soon after I was hired, I was given my first task to do by myself. In explaining the assignment to me, my boss said, 'This is not a difficult task, even a woman could do it.' That left me fuming."

Talk like this invites a woman's anger. Any man would become angered if a woman said something like that to him. Finding and using the talents of female employees can be a primary factor in the growth of a company. Men have to change the way they think about women, or women will never be able to display their true abilities in the company. Keep this in mind at all times.

Say "Thank You" Effectively and Often

Don't say, "Did you deliver the documents to the client?" when you can just as easily say, "Thank you for delivering the documents to the client." When served a cup of tea, you should say thank you first, then sip and comment that the tea is delicious.

Don't Praise a Particular Female Employee in Front of Everybody

If you ask one female employee to run errands for you on a regular basis, other female employees will start to think you're singling her out for preferential treatment. If you praise one woman, the rest will feel neglected and may bear a grudge. On the other hand, no one will notice if, in praising the entire team, you off-handedly mention the person you really wish to praise.

Don't Make Negative Comparisons

If you tell one woman that another would never make the sort of mistake she has just made, you run the risk of making her angry at your sexist remark, or destroying her confidence in herself. Don't bring up past mistakes when correcting mistakes that have just been made. Doing so only creates antipathy.

Don't Talk about Private Lives

Avoid talking about private matters in the office. It's none of your business when someone is going to get married or how old they are.

Don't Talk about Bonuses or Days Off

Often, just before bonuses are handed out, employees openly speculate about how much they'll get or talk about how they intend to spend their money. But you should remember that not all workers get the same treatment. Part-time workers and others who get paid by the hour may work in the same workplace but do not receive bonuses. Do not talk about bonuses in front of them.

Hourly workers are more likely than regular employees to come into the office even when they're not feeling well. It's irritating to them when regular employees call in sick because they're only running a slight fever. It's only natural for them to think that your taking off will increase the burden that they have to carry. Put yourself in the other employee's position and examine your behavior from their perspective.

Working with Older People

As a rule, when working with those who have more seniority than you, try not to talk about very important projects you're aware of or promotions within the company. Stick with topics like economics and social problems. And most importantly, be polite in speaking to them.

☛ Gifts and souvenirs are distributed by rank and age.

When you receive a seasonal gift from one of your clients or suppliers, don't open the package, because it's not yours to receive. Tell your boss who sent it to the company, and report it to the appropriate executive in the company. Also, when you receive a consumable souvenir from a business relationship, like cookies or sweets, get permission from your boss before opening the package and distributing treats to your coworkers. In sharing such things, always follow seniority order, and make sure that your boss receives some first.

Contribute to a Positive Mood on Company Outings

When we have a couple of drinks on a company trip or other event, some people forget they are employees of the company. But those who see this behavior don't forget. Being boorish or pushy only results in people losing trust and faith in you.

Don't just associate with your usual company friends. Try to speak to those you don't often have the chance to meet. You may find someone who is completely unremarkable at the office but who is excellent at sports. Cheer such people on, and you'll find the whole event will take on a livelier, more positive mood.

Participation in Events

When it comes to participating in company events, it's not good to be too passive, nor is it particularly good to appear too positive. Try to act as if you are enjoying the event, and this will help others enjoy it as well. Once you have learned to do this, you can enjoy it for its own sake.

Invitations to Others' Homes

☛ When visiting a colleague's home, it's not wise to tell his wife about the mistakes he makes at the office. She'll feel that no one respects her husband and that people laugh at him. What you think may be a very funny story can be misunderstood and have very undesirable consequences.

☛ Don't talk about other people's promotions. Wives tend to be more acutely sensitive about their husbands' careers and promotions than husbands themselves.

☛ If invited to dinner at someone's home, don't talk about it in front of someone who was not invited. He'll wonder why he was left out and will feel uncomfortable about it.

Watch Your Tongue When It Comes to Privacy

Mr. T, a lower ranking manager at a publishing house, was at his desk one morning, drinking a bottle of the ginseng and caffeine elixir that people take for a quick pick-me-up. He had been working several nights in a row overtime, and felt very tired. Just then his boss came in, and greeted him by saying, "Are you drinking that stuff again? Not another hangover?" Mr. T was infuriated all the more because his boss had just returned from a full week's vacation.

Mr. S, an employee of a medical equipment company, told his boss he had been diagnosed at a hospital as having a problem with his autonomic nervous system. His boss said, "In other words, it means you're lazy. Just stick to doing your job, and you'll be all right." Mr. S fell into a silent rage.

Department store employee Ms. I was told by her boss that, after four years of marriage, she ought to have had a baby. She felt she would have one when she was ready, and wished she could tell him that.

Mr. T, a real estate company employee, recalls an employee who came to work one morning with a story of a fire he had seen the previous night. "What a beautiful fire it was," he said. "I've never seen anything as exciting before as those flames. It was great." The fire had been at Mr. T's sister's home, and the family had lost everything.

CHAPTER 5

CONSIDERATION FOR FELLOW EMPLOYEES AT WEDDINGS AND FUNERALS

Behave Appropriately Even When Celebrating

☛ Whenever you're invited to a wedding ceremony, be sure to attend. Even when not invited, be sure to offer your congratulations.

☛ Be on your best behavior at receptions. People tend to look especially critically at tables full of noisy fellow employees.

☛ Don't try to outshine the main attractions. Dress appropriately.

☛ When asked to stand up and make a wedding speech, keep it to within three minutes. If asked to entertain, do so without hesitating.

Accept Congratulations without Hesitation

Marriage is, of course, a very private affair, but it is also a very important event in your life. Be straightforward in reporting your intentions to your boss or other people in the office, and accept their good wishes without hesitation.

☛ Start by letting your direct superior know. If you don't tell him and he learns about it from office gossip, he'll naturally feel disappointed and wonder why you didn't go to him first. Of course, you should chose the right moment. Avoid telling him during regular work hours. During lunch or after work is best.

☛ You'll be very busy taking care of all the details of the wedding, but under no circumstances should you take these matters to work with you. Take care of all such matters on your own private time.

☛ If you plan to invite people from work to your reception, remember you can't accommodate everyone. Invite those who have worked with you most closely. High-ranking people in your company will most likely have numerous invitations to receptions during the wedding season, so announce your intention to invite them to attend as early as you can. Also, after deciding who you wish to invite, get the invitations out as soon as possible. This helps to avoid confusion and hard feelings that result when people wonder if they are going to be invited or not.

☛ Often people ask colleagues from the company to be the master of ceremonies at their reception. Ask a superior to whom you feel close to play this role. You can also ask a friend to be your photographer.

Asking Your Boss to Be a Go-Between

The function of the go-between, who becomes the official emissary between the two families being united, is extremely important. Choosing someone to merely play the role on the day of the wedding, instead of being involved in the events from an earlier stage, can create misunderstandings and make certain people feel unhappy. When the couple decide to marry and wish to ask a boss to act as the go-between, they should consider the future of their relationship to that person in making the selection. Should you select your direct superior or his boss? If you decide to select your boss's boss or his boss's boss, you can smooth things over with your boss by getting him involved as the middle man to the higher executive you wish to act as go-between.

☛ Three months before the wedding, the couple should know whether the go-between will accept the role and then visit his home together with written personal histories, which will serve to introduce them to him.

☛ The go-between function is an important job. When considering how to express your gratitude to him, take into account the expense of his wife's kimono, the cost of the limousine and other expenses he has had to incur. After returning from the honeymoon, the couple should visit the go-between, bringing souvenirs, snapshots of their trip and also a gift of money to cover all of the expenses that were involved.

Thanking People After Your Wedding

☛ A small gift should be prepared for people who give a wedding gift but were not invited to the reception. They can also be invited to a small party the couple holds at their new apartment.

☛ The go-between should receive 100,000-200,000 yen, preferably in crisp new bills, enclosed in an appropriate envelope and delivered in person to his house.

☛ The master of ceremonies should be given about ten percent of what the go-between gets. If the emcee is a close friend, give a gift instead of money. If you plan to present the gift on the day of the ceremony, make sure it's not bulky. Inviting the person to one's home after returning from the honeymoon and then giving him the gift at that time is also a good idea.

☛ It's also wise to present money to others who helped out at the reception table or performed other important functions.

☛ For the person who acted as photographer, all expenses plus a gift of money should be calculated. In addition, it's a good idea to include several roles of film.

Heap Praise on the Couple

What to Give

Use whatever informal standard exists in your company in deciding how much you wish to give as a group. You can also ask the couple what they need: VCR, furniture, microwave oven or some other electric appliance. This is the more practical approach. Whatever you do, make sure the value of the gift is not too much more or less than the usual case at your company.

Choose someone who gets along with the prospective bride or groom to act as a gift coordinator, and have them ask what the person most wants and make the selection. If the item is large, rather than present it to the person at the company, it's better to give them a page from a catalog or some other document that shows what it is, and then have it delivered to the person's house the following day. The coordinator should give the person a list of everyone who contributed to the gift.

Invited to the Ceremony?

Be sure to identify the parents and family to congratulate them at the ceremony. This will make things go smoother at the reception.

☛ There are many ways to hold wedding ceremonies and receptions. Be sure to cooperate in creating the right atmosphere to conform to the particular ceremony chosen. For example, if it's a Christian ceremony where hymns are sung, you can try to mouth the words of the songs even if you don't know them.

☛ Often, people from the same company will be seated at the same table where they can enjoy talking with each other. But you can give offense to the family and other guests, by talking so much that you ignore the speeches that will be made in the course of the reception. Be careful to avoid laughing loudly or becoming absorbed in a conversation with other guests, as this will be disruptive to the general tone of things.

☛ Don't press the bride and groom to go to the customary informal party held after the wedding ceremony.

Speeches and Songs

☛ There are lots of true stories about people who, when asked to sing at a reception, chose songs about wives running off and leaving their husbands or other inappropriate themes. Songs should be upbeat.

☛ Don't make fun of the bride and groom's past or their mistakes in speeches about them. It can leave a bad taste in people's mouths.

☛ It's often fun to get four or five coworkers to sing a song together or do a short skit. This type of entertainment is very well received.

Support the Family in Their Grief

☛ There's no excuse for missing a funeral, no matter how busy you are.

☛ Express your deepest sorrow to the bereaved family. Company-related people should not become too conspicuous at funerals.

☛ Help the family, but leave all decisions about the type of funeral, the choice of the priest to perform the ceremony and other matters up to family.

Paint company executive Mr. S knows the value of keeping up-to-date records on who to contact in the event of an emergency. "One of our managers was killed in an auto accident. We tried calling his home but didn't get an answer. Someone remembered that his wife had recently gone back to work, but didn't know her employer. By going through old records, we were able to get her number from his family, but it took half a day to finally reach her."

When bad news comes suddenly, it's very difficult for the family to handle all the preparations for the funeral and other arrangements by themselves. Do your best to support them.

As Many People as Possible

Mr. S recalls another sad occasion. "When the wife of one of our executives died after an illness, we sent three male and two female employees right away to help with the wake. You'd be amazed at how many people it takes to handle the receiving line at a funeral."

☛ When an employee or his wife dies, send as many people as possible to help with the funeral.

☛ If a parent or child of an employee dies, take into consideration all the circumstances and then make a judgement about whether it's necessary to send people.

When an Employee Dies

☛ Make a prompt decision on whether a company funeral should be held and, if so, who should be the funeral coordinator. Of course, the family will decide on all matters related to the funeral, but it's customary, in such cases, to consult with the chief mourner and get his approval to send company people to handle the reception table, show visitors in and run errands. Messages of condolence should also be prepared promptly.

☛ Select a leader from among those sent to help out, and have him stay close to the chief mourner to make sure there is good communication on all arrangements. Consult the chief mourner on what type of flowers he would like the company to send to the funeral.

☛ It's very important to keep good records of who sent gifts of money, bouquets or other floral arrangements. Choose a reliable person to handle this task.

☛ Don't approach the casket unless requested by the family. When the family asks you to pay your respects to their loved one, approach the casket and bow once. When a family member removes the white covering cloth from the face of the deceased bow again this time more deeply, then bow to the family and go back to your seat.

☛ When visitors begin to arrive, things will get very busy. Running or hurrying in any way will detract from the proper atmosphere.

☛ Don't ask too much about the circumstances of the death or the illness that led to the death, as it will be painful for the family to retell the story. Company people should refrain from asking questions and observe silence. If asked to have a drink with others at the wake, limit your conversation to pleasant memories of the deceased.

☛ Once things settle down, helpers should avoid staying too long. The family needs time to say farewell to the deceased. Before going home, give all gifts of money that have been collected as well as the record of all visitors who have attended to the person in charge on the family's side.

After the Funeral

☛ A death of a spouse or child, unlike that of a parent who has lived a long life, will have an effect on a person's work. Be more considerate in such cases.

☛ Don't talk about the death with others at the company. It will be very unpleasant for the employee to hear even if you mean it to help him. Don't try to engage him in conversation about it unless he asks.

☛ If the person is very depressed or unable to sleep, have a friend whom he trusts approach him about it. They can suggest that he consult a doctor.

PART 3

SECRET TECHNIQUES FOR EXPANDING BUSINESS RELATIONSHIPS

CHAPTER 1

NEGOTIATIONS

The More You Know about People, the Better You'll Negotiate

- ☛ Your ability to negotiate is your most important asset in business.
- ☛ No one likes to be bargained down in negotiations. When negotiating always save the other person's face.
- ☛ The first ten seconds is the key. Make your strongest and clearest appeal to the other person in this window.
- ☛ Another way of negotiating is to overwhelm with kindness.
- ☛ In negotiating, you should approach from several different directions. Push here and pull there.
- ☛ People are responsible for what they say. Question the person aggressively to draw out his true intentions.
- ☛ You have achieved what you set out to do if, at the end, the other person agrees, in his own words, with the goals you set for the negotiation.

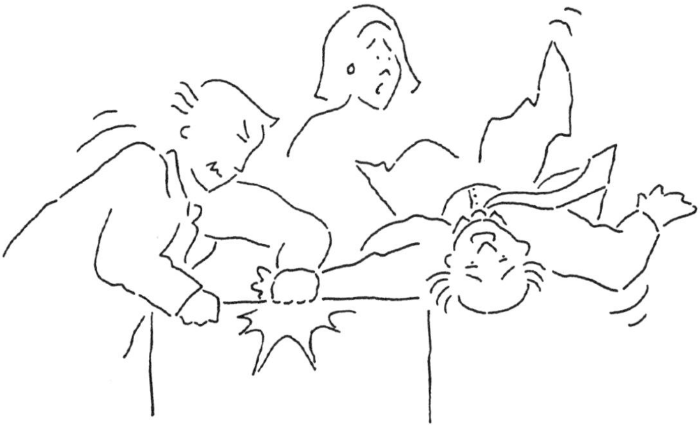

Negotiate with Passion and Sincerity

In business negotiating, people will routinely find one point after another difficult to agree on. To succeed in such negotiations, you need to show passionate commitment and sincerity to grab the attention of the other person and get him to listen to what you are saying. The techniques introduced here are tools to support you in this effort. Use them with careful consideration of the circumstances of each negotiation.

Never Talk the Other Side Down

In entering a business negotiation, remember that the basic premise is that there will be much bargaining in the course of it. In any negotiation, it's difficult to reach an agreement that's satisfactory to both sides. Always remember there's a next time and always make sure the other side doesn't lose face.

Construction company manager Mr. S describes how one negotiation produced an undesirable outcome when an employee ignored this important point: "One of my subordinates took our data and shoved it at the person he was negotiating with, and then made him accept a price increase by demonstrating the logic of our position. He won on that matter, but then we stopped getting work from that company. Although we won the negotiation, the results were negative for us. If you manage to win in a negotiation but the other person thinks you're arrogant or rude, then your victory is just an illusion."

Dazzle Them with Conversation

There are a variety of tools you can call on in negotiations. First, and foremost, is talk. This includes your facial expressions, choice of words, tone of voice, etc. You'll want to avoid making the client feel suspicious, uneasy or gloomy at any point in the conversation. Generally, speaking quietly is not a plus, but...

Grab Their Attention by Speaking Quietly

Director of sales promotion activities at a leading advertising agency, Mr. K, tells how he has used the technique to win accounts in many competitive presentations: "When my turn to talk comes, I speak more softly and in a lower voice than the person who came before me. In a way, you could say I almost whisper. It forces people to listen to what you're saying. They stop talking among themselves and give you their whole attention. Of course, you may get some complaints that people can't hear you, and you shouldn't try to use it every time."

Is There Really Such a Thing as a Halo Effect?

Because of their social position, family background or connections, there are some people who are regarded more highly than they really deserve to be. This psychological phenomenon is called the halo effect. No matter where you go, you'll find people who are unable to resist the appeal of this sort of opponent. If you are negotiating with someone with such a halo, the process will be made easier by involving an equally well-known person to help on your behalf.

"Let's" is the Way to Ask

By often saying "let's" to make suggestions in the negotiation, you can create a feeling of sharing and a mutual stake in the outcome of the discussion.

Let the Other Person Do the Talking

Say something to get the other person talking. Don't just force people to listen to you. If you structure your conversation properly and get the other person to talk, he'll take an interest in the subject even if he originally didn't want to.

The First 10 Seconds is the Key

When the negotiations start, the worst thing you can do is hem and haw nervously, flip the pages of your documents and then reach the end of what you have to say without communicating anything.

☛ Mr. Y, an auto sales executive who prides himself on excellent results, advises that the first ten seconds in which you meet the customer is the critical interval. And he has convinced his subordinates that he's right.

Let Them See, Read and Touch It

Negotiations aren't just carried on by speaking alone. You can convince the other person by using documents to cite data and refer to actual figures. You can also show the person photographs, slides and videotapes and let him or her hold miniature models in their hands. Make it a practice to employ techniques that appeal to all of the person's senses.

Use Psychology to Take the High Ground— It Makes Negotiations Go More Smoothly

There's No Better Target than Someone Who's Out

As strange as it seems, office automation equipment salesman Mr. K thinks there's no better prospect than someone who is away from the office when you make a sales call: "I leave a very politely worded message that I visited the person's office while he was out and that I'll come back again in the future. I may miss the person again, but I repeat the procedure until the person feels he has to meet me. By taking the initiative like this, the sales person is able to stand in a superior position and the conditions for negotiating become easier."

Replace One Intense Meeting with Five Laid-Back Ones

Another sales veteran has this advice: "I start by writing a letter and then follow up with a telephone call just about the time the letter should arrive. Often this is enough to convince the prospect. But if the answer isn't yes, I pay a call on the person.

"Because we have met face to face, it becomes that much easier to ask for the next meeting. After a few more low-key meetings, the prospect begins to feel enough pity for you that he begins to listen to what you have to say. At the point where you know each other by sight, it's possible to ask the tough questions that lead to a deal."

Techniques

There are several methods you can practice to add to your powers of persuasion in negotiations.

Imitate the Other Person's Speech Characteristics

In speaking with someone, it'll only be a few minutes before you notice something characteristic about the way the person talks. It may be that he has a weakness for using syllogisms, or that he favors words like "concept" and "risk" or that he has certain mannerisms. It's a safe bet that the other person thinks these characteristics are good. If you simply imitate his use of any of these characteristics, you can be pretty sure that his reaction will be, "This guy understands what I'm saying."

Prepare as Much Back-Up Information as Possible

Assemble as much easy-to-understand data as possible to back up the points you want to make. This can include everything from market surveys, statistics, quotes by authoritative sources and specialists, user evaluations of products and stories about first-hand experience with the product.

Things Sometimes Speak Louder than Words

Business accoutrements, like a fashionable briefcase, expensive fountain pen or "palmtop" computer, are noticed more than you would imagine. In choosing such items, try to make selections that say you are in tune with the times and have good taste. Of course, all business people should be well groomed and neat.

When Nothing Seems to Work

When the other person just won't say yes in the negotiation, try standing up, telling him you understand and thanking him very politely for his time. Sometimes this brings a person around when he is inclined to take the position you want but is still somewhat confused. As often as not, he'll ask you to wait and you can get down to business at last.

CHAPTER 2

NEMAWASHI FOR DECISION MAKING

This is the Core of Your Work

☛ Nemawashi is often translated as "laying the groundwork," but that phrase doesn't cover all of the aspects of what is a complicated, involved, but nevertheless all-important communication process. Doing the proper nemawashi requires that you get as much opinion input as possible, and then use it skillfully to achieve a successful outcome. It's your job to go about this task cheerfully, actively and precisely, soliciting opinions and ideas.

☛ First find out who are the right people to approach, put together a strategy that's in line with your objectives and then implement it while you have time.

☛ Never undertake a plan on your own. The ideal is to get your boss and your subordinates to feel a sense of participation in the planning of the job and then move together as a group on it.

☛ You should never stop listening to those who have a contrary opinion. If you manage to incorporate their opinions into your plan, it will be that much stronger.

☛ Approaching someone for nemawashi should be done in a natural, unaffected way and as conveniently for the other person as possible. Never announce that you have come to engage in nemawashi. That only turns people off.

☛ Showing sincerity and passion for your subject is the best weapon to make people truly agree with your idea. Always show respect to the person you're approaching.

☛ Even when you run into opposition to your ideas, hear the other person out. While listening to what they're saying, think of your next move.

☛ You have only failed completely when you leave someone feeling ill will toward you. Always leave the other person with a positive impression.

Nemawashi Without Thinking

Nemawashi is that Extra Consideration that Makes for a Good Job

Doing nemawashi is essential in everyday work, even when you're dealing with relatively minor tasks. Ridding the workplace of undesirable expressions like "That's the first I've heard of it" and "Why didn't someone ask me about it?" also depends on carrying on this process skillfully.

For example, when you're worried about finishing a difficult job by a particular deadline, don't keep it to yourself. Just by mentioning to your boss that you're having a hard time doing it because you don't have enough information can head off a reprimand later.

It's true that when you're working hard, you should be quiet and never give anyone the opportunity to think twice about your behavior, but it's also important to engage in nemawashi to protect yourself. Nemawashi is not something you need to consider unusual or difficult.

Nemawashi Today—Don't Overdo It

Nemawashi for Planning and Proposals:

1. First talk to your superiors and colleagues. This makes it possible to shift people away from seeing the idea as *your* plan and toward seeing it as everyone's plan. The secret is to take advantage of evening drinking sessions or lunches to pursue this topic. You can't just tell the other person, "This is how I incorporated your opinion in my plan," and then expect him to suddenly become enthusiastic about the idea. It doesn't happen that way. In contrast, if you keep the other person informed of your progress and ask for his opinions at each step of the way, you'll find that you may very well have made him a confirmed believer and solid supporter of your idea.

2. When support is beginning to materialize around you, it's time to consult a third party who is neutral on the question and has nothing to gain or lose from the outcome you desire. An objective opinion and good judgement should be prized. Besides giving you a valuable opinion, such people will also be frank about telling you who else must be consulted in the nemawashi process.

3. Next, you have to address those who have the opposite opinion or who are likely to experience some loss from the plan you are proposing. In particular, you have to make your case to the key

players in the company as well as those who are convinced the plan entails risks. As much as possible, you have to make your proposal reflect their ideas.

By starting your nemawashi on those around you at work, you'll widen your human network and get valuable information you might not otherwise have had access to. Use those contacts and that information in your next attempt at nemawashi and watch your success rate rise.

The Sooner You Begin, the Better

There are Three Stages in Nemawashi

☛ The first stage you have to be aware of is when to decide on the issue. As soon as the idea flashes in your mind, you naturally tell those around you in whom you have absolute confidence. You try to spread the feeling that your idea is something the company must implement. By doing this promptly and well, the job of nemawashi with others beyond your group will be made much easier.

By roughly sketching out an idea, and then asking others for their advice and help in fleshing it out, you'll give them a sense of "ownership" of the plan, and they'll feel they have a stake in making it successful. The number of supporters of the plan will multiply naturally, and the idea will start to move on to success.

☛ The next stage is for the production of planning documents. Enlist your boss and other interested parties and hold planning meetings. Work into your plans the results of all the opinions and problems that come up. This type of nemawashi is aimed at turning what had been "our plan" into "our department's plan."

☛ The last stage is that critical period just before the meeting to authorize that the plan takes place. This is when you should be dealing with the last opponents to your plan. Here, you have to discuss with passion and sincerity to win the day. If you have done sufficient nemawashi up to this point, the discussion at the meeting may very well tilt to your side.

There are cases, however, when the one who has implacably opposed the plan will continue to play the antagonist. At this point, you must patiently listen to his opinions. Even when the plan is about to be implemented, it's important to continue nemawashi with opponents and, as much as possible, have their opinions reflected in the plan. If the plan is eventually not executed properly, you run the risk of being accused of not having put enough effort into the process of reconciling the opponents.

Nemawashi Helps You to Grow

Think of nemawashi as a way to send out a signal to the organization that you're ready to set out on a course of action. In the process, you'll receive advice and opinions from a great variety of people, and no doubt some will encourage you to "stick to your guns." You'll become so involved in the process that, even if you wanted, you wouldn't be able to abandon the plan.

By concentrating all your attention on making up for the deficiencies in the plan and tackling the problems that appear, the plan will gradually become better and grow into something more meaningful. And, as it goes from being "our plan" to "our company's plan," you'll find that you, too, have grown in ways you hadn't considered. In short, nemawashi will turn something that had begun with a mere flash of inspiration into the power to reach a goal.

Nemawashi for Sure Success: Find the Key Man

The Right Time, Place and Occasion

Where does one start to launch a nemawashi campaign? A good standard would be to proceed in the following order:

1. Your direct superior and colleagues.
2. Your superior's colleagues and their superiors.
3. Specialists within the company.
4. Long-time employees with much experience..
5. People from the departments that will be affected by implementation of the plan.
6. Outside specialists and others regarded as authorities on the subject.

Of these categories, the people to whom you must pay the most attention are those in Groups 1 and 2. Whether it's a department head, section chief or manager, there exists a delicate power relationship between superiors and their subordinates. Not to upset that relationship requires discretion and more than a little consideration.

For example, if your department head has been newly appointed, begin nemawashi with more seasoned managers and section chiefs, since they can be very determined opponents. When necessary, you'll also want to recruit those who routinely help you in your office: your social group's leader, secretaries to

When You are Targeted for Nemawashi

- ***First, make sure you understand the broad outline of what the person is telling you. Be sure not to blurt out an opinion at this point.***
- ***Making up your mind about a plan is a lot easier once you know who is for it and who is against it and why.***
- ***If you have any doubts at all, don't get involved. Take some time to think the matter over carefully. Then, after hearing the ideas of both sides, look at it from the broadest perspective possible. Only then should you make up your mind.***
- ***When approached for nemawashi, be absolutely sure about the other person's position in the company, his power, standing, character and business sense.***

the board members and veteran female workers.

It's a good idea to construct a kind of chart in your mind to help you decide who is the most effective person to speak with first. As you go along, you can add to it or delete names as necessary, and gradually you'll see the direction of your strategy begin to emerge.

Putting It into Practice

☛ Remember to be flexible enough to choose a time when your target is relatively free of other tasks, has finished one job and is about to relax or has enough time to hear you out.

☛ When you come to do nemawashi, you must always maintain a humble position and modest bearing. Under no circumstances can you be perceived as arrogant.

☛ Begin by asking permission to speak to the target for just a short time; perhaps ten minutes or so will do. Then, concisely make your pitch, and politely ask for feedback.

☛ It is not particularly wise to ask whether the person agrees or disagrees at this point. The best course is to withdraw after very briefly asking for a general opinion about your idea or merely asking the other party to think it over.

☛ Never fail to be polite. Reminding people that you helped them recently on another matter, or resorting to intimidation by saying that everyone else in the department is for the idea will only be counterproductive.

☛ The key event in this process is the point when the other person tells you his opinion. Listen attentively, and encourage him to go on by telling him you understand what he is saying. All the while try to determine if this is a "honne" statement: that is, a statement that reflects his true position. A sure shortcut to making him an advocate for your idea is to persuade him to participate in the revising of your plans.

☛ There are also some who will agree with the rough outline of the idea but will find fault with some particular detail of it. Until you are sure they truly agree with you, it's best to insist that you fully intend to reconsider what they object to or that you will revise it later.

Turning Opponents Around You into Advocates

If the superior and colleagues you most want to support your idea stop you cold, be sure to reflect on your position carefully. After considering the reasons for their opposition, you have to confront the situation with acceptance. Go to those who opposed the idea and ask them why they were against it. It'll be hard to take, but have them detail their opposition point by point. Only when you have gone through this process do you have a chance of resolving the matter to your liking.

Useful Approaches in Nemawashi

- ***I need your advice.***
- ***Remember, I'll support your idea the next time, no matter what. Just help me this time.***
- ***This whole plan depends on you.***
- ***This plan won't succeed without you.***
- ***Thank you for your very valuable advice. Let me think about it and I'll come back to you again.***

A Few Psychological Ploys

☛ ***The "Always" Tack***

When enlisting support, tell your targets that you're grateful to them for "always" helping you and "always" responding to your requests. In the human mind, there is a desire to maintain some

Where People Sit Can Tell You Where They Stand

When you are doing nemawashi at a coffee shop or restaurant, where people sit can give you an idea as to what their positions on your idea are.

When He Arrives Before You

☛ A person who sits close to the door is probably not going to be very patient. Keep your explanation short and to the point.

☛ Someone who sits in the middle will tend to be self-centered and very willing to reveal his feelings. You don't have to be forceful with nemawashi for this person.

☛ The person who takes a seat in the rear wants to settle down to hear your plan. Take your time in making your case to this person. He's ready to hear you out.

When He Arrives After You

☛ If he takes a seat facing you, it means he is willing to listen until he understands your point.

☛ If he sits at an angle, you can assume he won't go along with your idea. Be careful in dealing with him.

type of consistency in our behavior. By stressing their positive response to you and using the word "always," you trigger a desire to respond the way they always do.

☛ ***A Smile and a Serious Expression***

Starting out and finishing up with a smile on your face is not the best approach. At some point, your facial expression should become intense as you describe your plan without hiding your enthusiasm for it. Even when you begin with a frank and open explanation of the plan, it's most productive to switch to an absolutely serious look when it comes to pressing the point.

☛ ***Dealing with Hardheads***

When you have to deal with those who stubbornly refuse to change their opinion no matter how convincing your arguments are, there's usually no point in a frontal attack. In fact, insisting on your viewpoint will only make them more attached to their opinion. Hear their ideas out first. Only when you do this and understand what points they are trying to make will you be closer to reaching your goal. At that point, even if someone still opposes your plan, you will have made progress, because, like most people, in the future he'll be more likely to listen to those who understand him and his ideas.

☛ ***When It's Completely Impossible***

When you are clearly turned down, try asking how you can revise the plan so that it won't be so objectionable to that person. Since he has just finished refusing you, you can assume he may feel sorry enough for you that he'll give you some good ideas and hints for the future. If that fails, you haven't lost anything by trying. If, after trying all of these tacks, the person is still intractable, it's best to withdraw and see what happens.

CHAPTER 3

3

THE HUMAN NETWORK: JUST LIKE PLAYING CATCH

☛ In building your network, always calculating the value of each contact means certain failure.

☛ You can't build a network if you go by titles alone.

☛ Look for those who have useful information or wisdom to share with you. This becomes the basis for an easygoing give-and-take relationship.

☛ Don't rush things. When the other person is busy ,wait for the next opportunity. Your relationship is built on your respect for the other person.

☛ If there's a break in your relationship, look at it as a chance to make your ties even stronger. Then throw all your energy into repairing it.

You Know You're Succeeding When Someone Says: "I Owe You a Favor"

People with Networks are Almost Always Popular

Mr. M, a manager at a large electronics manufacturer, tells this story about the value of the human network:

"My boss, a senior manager who I had only known as a very dedicated, 'all-business' executive, took me by complete surprise not long ago. 'They tell me you want to find out how housewives feel about your new product,' he said. 'I'll introduce you to a wonderful woman who heads a housewives group.' As it turned out, she was a member of his tennis group.

"It seems that his circle of friends was much wider than I had ever imagined. When one of our fellow employees suddenly collapsed at work, the boss had him taken right away to a brain surgeon who was a personal friend of his. It was a very serious cerebral hemorrhage, but the patient's life was saved because the right specialist could treat him immediately. You can really depend on a person like that, a person who has such a wide network of friends."

It shouldn't be surprising that Mr. M says he wants to learn from his boss and develop his own strong human network.

Start Your Network with Those Closest to You

Building a network of connections proceeds based on the experiences you've had and your own temperament. You'll see its true value when you are confronted with unexpected situations or difficult problems. You should begin your network by doing a little bit of research and mapping out the power relationships in your company, pinpointing where the reliable pipelines of information are and how they are connected.

Don't omit any of the following from your map:

☛ Colleagues and senior executives that your direct superior admires.

☛ The boss of your workplace and the main veteran employees.

☛ Employees you get along with who were hired in the same year as you.

☛ People from other departments who work closely with you. (Include secretaries, general affairs people, receptionists and security staff as well.)

☛ Outside consultants and specialists.

The Right Preparation

If, in building your network, your personal stake or motives in doing so become obvious, you will most certainly fail. Begin by going over the following checklist:

☛ Are you useful to the person you want in your network? Start providing him with information he finds of interest. When he's in a bind, help him out. Whatever you do, always add to the number of favors you have done for him.

☛ Does the person expect something of you? Always keep your antenna up to catch information that might be of use to him. Try out interesting things and places, and vacuum up stories and other useful information. After awhile when a question comes up, he'll point to you and say, "Ask him, he'll know."

☛ Can you ask questions bluntly? Just giving an opinion or making a guess is a hindrance to business. You have to be blunt about the information that you want. This is the root of communication and is an important part of building networks of connections in business.

Doing Favors is Only Half the Job

Mr. O, a public relations manager at a large fuel processor, explains his approach to network building: "There's no value in pretending to know it all and doing things to impress those around you. What's essential is your work everyday. What is valuable is to have a lot of people who think you owe them favors.

"First find someone to ask a favor of and then return it. Go through the process again. This is the trick to it. You'll find that through your daily work you'll build up a proper network naturally."

Always Reevaluate

In reevaluating your network, start by checking your business card file, the list of people in the company, greeting cards you've received during the year and cards announcing reassignments and other personnel changes. You'll notice that there are people you haven't been in touch with, or some from whom you've been maintaining a respectful distance for one reason or another.

If it's a relationship that you want to continue, then you can either telephone or write a short letter or post card to them to let them know how you are. But the sooner you get in touch the better. And make a mental note to do something everyday to stay in touch with and expand your network.

☛ Participate actively in clubs and sports inside and outside the company. Win the favor of people in these groups and they will elect you to positions with more responsibilities.

☛ Get as active as you can in Go, Shogi, fishing, golf and hiking activities and expand your interests. Those without such interests will not be able to build the structure for a network of connections.

☛Chance encounters are also important. You can add people you never thought of before to your network by taking the opportunity to greet people or striking up conversations during work hours at the office, in the elevators and in the cafeteria.

Using Third Parties

Mr. I, an information services company salesman, tells the following story:

"I wanted to ask Mr. K, an engineer, about a revolutionary new data transmission system, but I knew he was terribly busy. So I asked my superior who often visited his office to help me. I didn't know what to think when I was soon invited to join a study group that Mr. K himself led."

As a result, not only was Mr. I enlightened about the data transmission system, but his reputation within the company soared. If you want to put a certain person into your network, it's useful to take a roundabout method and find a third party associated with him. Tell the third party how much you admire the one you are targeting and he'll definitely pass on your praise. This, more often than not, will ease the way to getting the meeting that you seek.

Making a Human Network File

☛ Use business cards you collect. Jot notes down on the card, including the day you met the person, what the circumstances were, any impressions, the person's interests and any other useful information. By routinely going through the cards and reviewing these notes, you might be able to fill in a hole in your network.

☛ Keep a good file of year-end greeting cards and cards announcing personnel shifts, and try to keep up with the current status of those people. This can be useful when you're looking for ways to reestablish communications with them or if you need to buy gifts.

☛ Keep a good address book and diary.

In it, keep notes on the family structure, interests, birthdays, favorite foods and drinks of the most important people in your network. Also, every three to five years start a "Remember Book," one of those diaries that gives the date at the top of the page only but not the day of the week.

Here, you can keep a handy record of who you had a lunch date with or to whom you gave a gift on that day.

If you are faithful in writing in entries, it can become an excellent history of your relationships.

Never Ask Too Much — Don't Become a Burden

The trick to keeping your network intact over the years is to maintain the proper distance between contacts. If you try to step too close and end up giving offense, you can change the relationship into an unhappy one.

☛ Don't contact people when they're busy, especially during budget settlement season.

☛ Don't appear conspicuous when thanking anyone for documents. It creates a burden for both people if others in the company think that they're too friendly.

☛ Be cautious about introducing people or bringing anyone along to meet the important people in your network. If you're asked for an introduction by someone, think long and hard about whether the asker is really a useful person before you bring the two together.

☛ Bragging about your network will only detract from it. By clumsily revealing yourself in this way, you can invite unwanted speculation and resentment.

Mr. S, an executive at a large electronics manufacturing company, says he almost found this out the hard way: "I attended a study meeting at which someone from a rival company was present. We soon started to chat about the atmosphere within our companies. When I reported this conversation to my boss, he complimented me for making this connection and told me to build on this relationship carefully. But at the same time, he warned me not to mention it to anyone else since they might accuse me of leaking information."

To Strengthen Your Network

☛ Send friendly letters or postcards to your network whenever you travel.

☛ When you travel on business to the provinces, bring back their favorite foods as souvenirs.

☛ Send presents on important birthdays, their children's admission to schools, graduations and other happy occasions.

☛ Rather than sending the ordinary end-of-the-year and midsummer gifts, you communicate your feelings much better by sending gifts of fresh food at the peak of the season.

Thanks for an Introduction

Toy manufacturing executive Mr. T remembers being very grateful for a particular introduction:

"When the problem came up, I went through all my connections to find someone to give me an introduction to an attorney who specialized in overseas litigation. Thinking that some sort of gift was called for to express my gratitude, I gave a present to the person who introduced us, and asked him to give it to the attorney. 'I can't accept this for him,' he said. 'If I give it to him, he might think that I'm getting some sort of kickback from this and get angry at me.' Well, I finally sent it directly to the lawyer myself. But when I started out, I had no idea things would become that difficult."

You Run a Certain Risk

In your human network you meet people, share something with them, meet them again and repeat the cycle, deepening the relationship. But it's possible that the reverse can happen. Cracks can develop in the relationship over something trivial and can lead to some risk for both parties.

In all relationships, there is an invariable four-step process: separation, risk, restoration to the former state and reinforcement. People's opinions are different (separation), they clash (risk), they restrain their views, approach each other again and repair the relationship. If, for example, you see risk arising in the connection, view it as part of the process and you'll be able to achieve an even stronger relationship later.

To overcome the risk:

☛ Try to find something in the person's argument that you can agree with, conceding that on such and such point he is right.

☛ If you are guilty of any offense, admit it forthrightly and apologize.

☛ Once you see that the other person recognizes his faults in the argument, it's more considerate to avoid any reference to them beyond that.

Build Your Network with Younger People, Too

Within your network, you'll no doubt have people with less power than yourself. You'll make a serious error if you try to drop them from your network because you think they won't be useful. As they grow, they can develop into important connections for you. For the time being, such younger members of your network are an unknown quantity, but, if anything, that should make it all the more interesting to cultivate them.

People who are tough on others but easy on themselves can't build human networks. Those who demand more of themselves and are considerate of others have what it takes to create unlimited connections. The more tolerant you are of others, the more likely you'll be to meet greater, more influential people.

CHAPTER 4

REFUSING

☛ Refusing basically means you are going to damage the pride of the other person. Be respectful and try to help him save face.

☛ Your attitude should be that the reason you have to decline is not the other person's fault, but rather because of your own lack of resources or power.

☛ When saying good-bye after refusing, talk about something else that you can both laugh about. Don't leave any negative feelings after parting.

☛ When you have to decline an invitation from your boss, don't forget to thank him for thinking of you.

☛ When you decline an invitation to entertain others with a song or skit, the trick is to do it with humor but firmly.

☛ Decline clearly and firmly when approached for loans or to become a co-signer for someone else's loan.

☛ You do yourself credit when you decline to give information about your company. Also, you can't afford to let anyone think you'll help with matters related to hiring.

Firmly, Gently and Without Hurting the Other Person's Feelings

Whether They Get Angry or Understand — All Depends on How You Refuse

Clearly but Without Hurting their Pride

Everyday, we are asked by others to do things, or invited to take part in different activities. While it would be wonderful if we could do everything we are asked, the reality is that we just can't. There are many times that we have to decline. But declining can be remarkably difficult.

Ms. I, the director of the women's clothing department of one large department store, had to refuse to accept an item of clothing one customer wanted to return. Ms. I could see that the goods had been dry-cleaned. This is how she phrased her refusal: "It's obvious that someone in your family mistakenly sent this to the cleaners. Unfortunately, we don't accept goods for return that have been dry-cleaned."

Ms. I chose this way to express her will in order not to expose the customer's lie about the goods and to save her pride. At the same time, she was unmistakably clear in her refusal. In business, it is wise to maintain this spirit.

☛ Everyone feels a certain amount of unpleasantness when refused, so try to keep the amount of hurt to a minimum when you have to decline someone's offer. Remember, there's no limit on the number of times you can say, "I'm sorry." Say it often and with feeling.

☛ Saying "no" flatly and leaving it at that is just not enough. You have to let the other person know that you are declining because of your lack of power or resources or because of circumstances unrelated to him.

☛ Listen well to what the other person is asking you to do. Nod and interject "I understand" where appropriate. He should be able to feel your sincerity.

☛ If you consider that you might very well be in the other person's place at some point, you will treat him with politeness. Once the main topic has been covered, switch to a lighter subject that you can both enjoy and then part on an upbeat note.

What Female Employees Would Most Like to Decline

- ***Being asked to go out and buy six different kinds of box lunches for male employees in the office.***
- ***Being asked to make meaningless changes in word-processed drafts by men who are too lazy to do it themselves. What a waste of time!***
- ***Being asked out for a drink by a male employee with the line, "I'll teach you everything you have to learn about this business." Can't you teach at the office? (This complaint comes most often from new female employees.)***
- ***Being asked to make copies for a male employee who stands by and chats as we run the pages through the copier. We women have our own work to do.***

There are Many Occasions for Refusals

Declining Invitations from Superiors

When a boss asks a subordinate to have a drink with him, it might mean no more than that. When possible, the subordinate will want to comply, but there are times when he can't. In declining, be clear and to the point, but have a good excuse. You can embellish the excuse with a little exaggeration or a white lie or two if necessary. Afterwards, be sure to express thanks for the invitation and show regret that you couldn't make it.

Declining Invitations to Perform

Of course, when invited to sing or perform a skit, you should accept. But there are those who for whatever reason can not bring themselves to do it. When asked, they should refuse firmly but with a bit of humor. For example, you can make a show of begging everyone's forgiveness for not being talented enough to perform before the group. This doesn't throw a wet blanket on the mood of the event. If you only weakly say you don't think you're any good, people will interpret it as modesty and encourage you all the more. If everything fails, you can do imitations of animals or you can ask someone who excels at performing to give you a hand.

Declining Presents

If it's not clear why someone is offering you a gift, refuse it, explaining that the company's policy doesn't allow you to accept such presents. If you refuse and don't add the reason, the giver may feel he's been insulted.

Second Parties

Formal events are often followed by less formal parties that begin much later in the evening. If you have an important job the following day or you're not feeling well, don't be afraid to say you have other things to do. As you leave, tell everyone that you had a wonderful time and wish you could stay longer, but don't let anyone talk you into staying. Say good-bye to each person. If they've been drinking for awhile, they won't mind your slipping out.

Smoking

When the other person offers you a cigarette, it means he wants to smoke. These days, people are sensitive about smoking, and simply saying that no, you don't smoke can actually cause offense. Smokers interpret that to mean, "Do you mean that you still smoke?" To avoid problems, decline politely and offer an ashtray, showing that while you don't smoke, you don't mind if others do.

Breaking Off Relations

You may think you'll never do business with a certain person or company again, but before you say that or put it in writing, think twice. Companies are people organized for the

• Having to get tea for male employees who then order us to clear away the tea cups. Why can't they take their own tea cups back to the kitchen?

• Being required to stay after hours for overtime that drags on and on. We'd love to refuse to stay.

• Being asked to fawn over an especially good client. We were hired as employees of the company, not hostesses.

• Being asked to apologize for a male employee because women are better at it. If it's your mistake, you apologize for it.

• Having to tell callers that male employees are out of the office when they're not, which can be infuriating.

purpose of doing business. They operate as organizations. Try to think whether the problem is the company or just one person in the company whom you just can't stand. Try to look at the problem from the larger perspective and then decide if it's worth breaking off the relationship.

If after all that, you still decide that you don't want to do business with such an organization, consider that it's a bit old-fashioned to cut off the possibility of future business. It's much better to let business relations slowly come to an end without a dramatic finish. In any case, it's wise to avoid any bitter break in relations that results from an individual's personal decision made in anger.

When it Comes to Refusing, Don't Drag Things Out

Information Leaks

When asked about new business, personnel changes, who the company is entertaining, new products or any other such sensitive information, play dumb. Or, you can simply let the other person know that you don't want to talk about the subject. Everyone knows how important information is in business, so if you refuse to divulge it, you will only increase the respect others will have for your trustworthiness.

Co-Signing Loans

Don't do it. You can refuse by simply saying you're not able to do it. Probably the one who asks will have some tie of obligation to you, but simply saying "I'm sorry, I can't" should make clear how you feel about it. Someone who still persists at that point will be fairly desperate. Continuing the discussion will almost certainly result in ill feelings between the two of you.

Loans

When asked, just say that it's your policy to neither borrow from nor lend to friends. If you think about the loan and then tell the person that you can't later, he'll naturally think you believe he won't pay back the loan. This leaves bad feelings in the relationship.

CHAPTER 5

APOLOGIZING

> ☛ When apologizing, don't offer excuses.
>
> ☛ Being able to readily say "I'm sorry, I was wrong" is the mark of a good business person.
>
> ☛ When apologizing, you should know what made the other person angry.
>
> ☛ The worst kind of apology is one in which you either hesitate or don't come to the point.
>
> ☛ Sometimes no apology can be the best apology.
>
> ☛ Apologies reveal your weaknesses. Keep them short to prevent leaks to outsiders.

The One Who Takes a Scolding Well Does his Job Well

Sometimes You Have to Sacrifice Your Own Pride and Go Hat in Hand

If you spill a cup of coffee you naturally apologize for your mistake. In business, the sad truth is that you often have to apologize for things you didn't necessarily do. When apologizing, first decide what is the objective of the apology:

☛ Maintaining a smooth-running business relationship.

☛ Keeping or reviving a good relationship with a key person in your network.

☛ Where someone is injured or suffers some sort of damage, making sure that the demand for payment will be as small as possible.

Sometimes you'll need to take a cool, detached approach. At other times, you can do a study of the other person's personality as you keep in mind why it is that you must apologize. If you can truly understand what it is to apologize, you won't have any problem knowing the when, where, why and how of apologizing. In fact, you may even be able to apologize from the heart.

For Missed Deadlines, Apologize ASAP

Use Long-Range Timing

Mr. M, a manager in the advertising department of a certain automaker, tells this story: "The production people turned out a good plan for proceeding, so I asked them to submit an advertising plan to me in memo format. But on the appointed day not only was the memo not delivered to me, but the one responsible for producing it was not even at his desk. I didn't even get a phone call from him."

The next day, Mr. M got a phone call from the person in charge, making excuse after excuse for not meeting the deadline. This made him even angrier. After listening to what the ad man had to say, he called off the project and stopped dealing with the agency. The reason he was so angry was because the agency had caused him a great deal of embarrassment. He had believed in their idea and thought he would receive the memo on the day as promised. Expecting to receive it, he had gone ahead and scheduled an internal meeting to go over the plan.

If the agency had called him a few days earlier to say that the plan was running late, it would have been possible to do something to head off the trouble. As it happened, the episode resulted in the worst possible outcome. In apologies for missed deadlines, timing is everything. Apologize to the other person before he feels the impact of the missed deadline, and do whatever he asks.

Your Subordinate's Mistakes are Your Mistakes— Apologize for Them Without Reservation

Mr. G, who is now a manager at a company that manufactures painting robots, recalls a lesson a client taught him early in his career: "I gave my subordinate the job of producing a chart to show our running costs. To make sure he could get the job done by the deadline, I provided him with documents he would need and made sure he had enough time to do the work. I even did some of his other jobs, but even so he couldn't finish it. Of course, I went to the client to apologize, and because I felt so bad about it I began to complain about the subordinate.

"'That's fine. I can wait another few days,' he said. 'But nobody wants to listen to you complaining about your subordinate.' I was so embarrassed I broke out into a cold sweat."

Apologizing for someone else is not easy. Here are some tips to keep in mind to make it less difficult:

☛ In business, one company deals with another company. When there is a failure, there are neither bosses nor subordinates. Everyone shares in the responsibility and apologizes for the failure.

☛ A company is respected for its ability to work as an organization. You deny your company's organizational ability when you engage in defending your actions apart from those of the company. This results in damage to the credibility of the company.

☛ Apologize unreservedly for clear-cut failures or broken promises.

Sometimes an Abject Apology is Necessary—and Sometimes Not

Sincerity is the Best Policy

When you have made a mistake or caused injury or damage to another person, a forthright apology, without excuses, is absolutely necessary.

☛ For missed deadlines or failures: "It was all my fault. I regret having caused you so much inconvenience. I'm very sorry."

☛ For misunderstandings: "I should have asked your opinion first. I'm truly very sorry."

Apologies should be accompanied by a deep bow. To express the proper degree of sincerity, your apology should be spoken clearly and slowly so as to be easily understood by the other person. In business, there is no place for perfunctory, meaningless apologies. There is no way to meet a person's deeply felt, true anger except with a deeply felt apology from the heart.

Apologizing for Injury Or Damage

1. First, make a sincere effort to clarify the facts of the matter, and then try to do whatever you can to lower the compensation you'll have to pay. Even if the other person is still angry, stay firm in saying that you wish to accept the full responsibility for the matter.

Letters of Apology

Whenever you miss a deadline to deliver a product, make errors in calculation or receive complaints over problems with quality, you may be requested to write a letter of apology. The point in the exercise is to recognize your own faults right away and write the letter promptly. The letter should be politely phrased and should specify how you intend to deal with the problem.

Sometimes compensation for damages is requested by the other party, so be very cautious in how you write the letter. Take into account what type of person the other party is. In certain cases, it is wise not to put an apology into writing.

2. If it appears that you are in some way or other trying to evade your responsibilities, the other person will sense it and will most likely further harden his attitude toward you. The first apology should be made as soon as possible. Accept full responsibility openly to avoid further alienating him.

3. Depending on the circumstances of the injury, you may be required to write a report and a member of your upper management may have to make a visit to the victim to apologize. Take into account all the circumstances and act promptly.

4. When there is fault on both sides, both parties have to talk objectively about how to settle the matter. Rather than the two principles in the matter, it's often more desirable to have their bosses meet to talk since they will be familiar with the course of the problem and will be able to speak with a degree of responsibility.

Making Your Apologies an Asset for Everyone in the Company

It's human nature to want to cover up mistakes and apologies. When you have caused injury to another company, however, it's important to reevaluate the organizational structure of your company.

☛ The section responsible for the damage should gather the other sections that had something to do with the failure that led to the injury, and then together examine the course of the problem in detail and identify each of the factors that contributed to the problem.

☛ They should study whether there were any problems in the reporting system that may have led to the damage. They should also study whether the problem may have arisen because the wrong person was assigned to do the job.

☛ When there is a problem related to a lack of understanding of the costs involved in a certain job or a lack of motivation to do the job, they should reflect on why these problems arose.

After taking these steps, report to your client, if necessary, on what you have done. This can be the occasion to win more business from the client or simply a chance to reassure him that it will not happen again.

It's a good idea to follow up on each of your mistakes on a daily basis in this way. If you don't understand what you're doing wrong, you're liable to make the same mistakes all over again. And if you always have to apologize for the same sort of mistakes, you'll never get anywhere.

Become Good at Accepting a Dressing Down

The director of general affairs at a large bank, Mr. R, explains how to take a scolding: "Subordinates who are good at accepting a dressing down or skillful at apologizing always will rise in the company. You'll see them really criticized by a boss one day, and then the very next day they'll come in as cheery as if nothing at all had happened. Instead of sulking, they'll greet their boss with an apology for their mistakes and a word of thanks for correcting them. They bow and say that it was a good experience for them. These are the sort of employees I want to keep an eye on."

Whatever you do, don't agonize very long over being scolded. If you're always wearing a gloomy expression, your boss won't think any the better of you, and your colleagues will come to dislike you. Remember that apologizing can be the occasion for a good deal of self-growth.

Apologies that are Subtle

At one time or another, you may have told someone that you could never possibly like them. But as time passes, you discover that he or she was not such a bad person at all. Rather than approaching the person with an outright apology for misjudging him, it might be a better idea to use the office grapevine to communicate your feelings. Praise him to a third person, and the news of it will definitely flow back to him.

☛ When your boss takes care of a mess that you're responsible for, he is treating your failure as his own. Such cases are not rare. It's best to apologize to your boss promptly, and then try to make it up to him by working even harder at your job.

☛ There are also times when, no matter how much you apologize, you just can't put things right with another person. Take your time in rebuilding the relationship. Write reports of interest to that person frequently, collect information for him from outside the company, keep good files on such data and occasionally place it on his desk without making a fuss over it. Stick with the program until he recognizes your sincerity.

CHAPTER 6

TROUBLE

Stick Together

☛ It's important to maintain solidarity to deal with outside problems that require a prompt response.

☛ If you don't put the safety of your customers and visitors ahead of everything else, you will be stuck with a deservedly bad reputation.

☛ Keep a tight rein on your emotions. It's necessary to be able to coolly consider what the next step is.

☛ Maintain firmness in dealing with uninvited guests. Stay composed.

☛ As much as possible, don't mention anything about the problem. If it becomes a story that people repeat and laugh over, it could be embarrassing for your company.

☛ Keep in mind that trouble doesn't necessarily happen to other people alone. Study how problems are resolved and maintain an interest in collecting know-how on solutions.

☛ This is the era of risk management. The company and its employees should be ready to deal seriously with risk.

Coping with Traffic Accidents: Act Quickly but Keep Your Head

Trouble has many faces. If there is solidarity among the employees of a company, they can pool their resources to keep the impact of the trouble to a minimum and eventually overcome it.

Employee Traffic Accidents

When an Employee is Hit by a Car While Out of the Office on Business

☛ If possible, someone who has dealt with accidents in the past should be put in charge. Depending on the condition of the employee, there most likely will have to be someone to deal with handling the accident and seeing to it that the employee is admitted and well taken care of at the hospital. It's wise to assign the job to two people.

☛ First, check to make sure that the employee's family has been properly notified. If it appears that they have not, you and your staff should do your best to contact them about it as soon as possible.

☛ The employee who is sent to deal with the accident or hospitalization should make an accurate report on the situation, inform the company and be ready to follow instructions the company may give him.

☛ If the injured person had an important business meeting or trip on his calendar, make the necessary notifications, but don't appear disorganized about it. Find out the nature and severity of the employee's injuries before making these calls. Remember that even if the employee is not to blame for the accident, generally speaking it will be perceived as something negative about your company.

☛ When an upper-level executive or key man on a major project is involved in an accident, there are times when it will be necessary to keep it a secret as long as the injuries are not serious. Wait for instructions from the executive responsible for the matter, and refrain from leaking the news to outsiders.

When Employees on Company Business Cause Traffic Accidents

☛ Send someone who has experience in handling accidents to the scene right away.

☛ The employees on the scene should put priority on saving lives. Even if you think that it's necessary, do not try playing the defender on behalf of the employee. Taking photographs of the scene while victims are still there detracts from the dignity of your company. On the scene of an accident, you are a representative of your company, and should act with the proper bearing and composure.

☛ If you hear that an accident has occurred while you're outside the office on business, don't spread the news within the company even when you run back to the office to report it.

☛ If someone is injured because of the fault of an employee, the appropriate executive should visit the injured person in the hospital to show the company's sincerity in the matter.

Be Prepared

Procedures for Handling the Accident Should be Clear

To avoid confusion over a person's whereabouts in the event of an accident, each section should have a board on which the employee writes where he is going and for what purpose each time he or she leaves the office. Also, the telephone numbers of all clients should be listed and kept in a place that is easily accessible to all employees in case of emergencies. Such routine precautions can mean the difference between a prompt response and confusion in an emergency situation.

Using Company Cars

Maintain a schedule for using company cars. It should be clear from one glance at the schedule who is driving which car and when he or she will be returning to the office. Choose a manager who will be held responsible for the use of company cars. If responsibility is not clarified or if the use of the cars is not strictly regulated, the situation will quickly deteriorate. If you let employ-

ees take cars out for inappropriate reasons, you'll never know where the cars are when you need them.

We often hear of cases in which an employee injured in an accident had been carrying an important contract that was to be delivered the following day. Or that the vehicle was on its way to deliver several million dollars in valuables. Prompt follow-up in such cases can decide the fate of a company.

3

A Customer Who Comes to the Office to Make Baseless Complaints

Should One Person Take Care of It or Several?

There are occasionally customers who will yell at employees and upbraid the company in front of other customers. There are times when you wonder if their anger is justified or whether they have some other objective in mind. In any case, it should be arranged beforehand that such people will be taken to a reception or conference room, where an executive of the company will objectively listen to their complaints. Veteran executives from the general affairs department are the right sort of person to handle this job.

One such veteran, Mr. W, a senior executive at a fuel oil company, gives this advice: "Show them into a conference room as you would anyone else. When you think someone is justified in his anger at the company, meet him and have several other people from the company at your side. They can act as witnesses so that you can avoid confusion later about what was said and what wasn't. On the other hand, if the customer's intention is to extort from us or threaten us, I try to meet him one on one."

Of course, when what angered the customer results from mismanagement, there should be several employees to meet with the customer, since they will all play a role in repairing the damage done.

Another veteran general affairs executive from a telecommunications company, Mr. G, explains the difficulty of dealing with a customer whose real intention is extortion: "The most desirable way to deal with these people is have two people meet with them, one of whom will act very hostile to the customer while the other will be friendly. Whenever the first gets visibly angry about the customer's complaint, the other tries to remove the chill from the atmosphere."

There's really no "best way" to deal with such attempts, but of the 16 general affairs experts polled, a majority agreed on the following:

☛ No matter how much the customer pushes, don't ever offer them money.

☛ Never sign any documents or make any kind of promises.

Anticipate Problems and Deal with Them Promptly

Those who come to make threats will usually start by complaining about shortcomings of the company's products or services, the way an ordinary dissatisfied customer would. The basic rules for dealing with such complaints are:

☛ Maintain the same attitude you would take toward any other customer.

☛ Hear the person out. Let him say whatever he wants to say. If you do this properly, you can get a good idea of what his objective really is.

☛ When you offer to take the appropriate steps to remedy the situation but the customer doesn't accept, don't offer anything else. Instead, ask what it is the company can do to satisfy him, and make your decision about what he's after on this basis.

☛ Once his demands are clear, spare no effort in refusing. When you feel there is no way you can refuse this person enough, end the meeting abruptly.

Often, the one who is threatening will complain that the company is avoiding its responsibility by sending someone to deal with him who does not have the authority to make a decision. He'll then demand that a higher executive meet with him. If you refuse to accommodate his request, he'll change his attitude and complain that you are being rude to him. It can become a real war of nerves.

Winning in a War of Nerves

When you're in that kind of situation, how do you come through successfully? One manager who specializes in resolving such matters has offered some very simple advice: "Once you say something, you don't change it, no matter what happens. This is how you can avoid being taken advantage of by the other person. Repeat as many times as necessary, 'What I told you before still stands.'

"After someone has been visibly angry for about two hours or so, he becomes fatigued. Listen to the person for two hours. Then try to change the mood a bit by introducing other topics. At this point, he will realize that you're not going to move an inch from your position and more often than not will just give up."

Threats from Unidentified Sources

Threatening letters and phone calls, if they continue, can have an effect on employee morale and can eventually have an impact on your business. Here's what to do:

☛ If the threats don't let up and, in fact, get worse, consult the police.

☛ When a threatening letter is delivered, don't throw it away even if it makes you upset to think of it. Put it aside. For threatening calls, make records of the time and nature of the call and tape them, too, if possible.

☛ Becoming fearful or upset about threats plays into the hands of the person making them. It's best to deal with such matters in a cool and detached manner. If it appears that the threats will continue for quite a while, assign someone to handle all threats and materials related to them. This prevents confusion in your response.

Mounting a Defense Against Threats

☛ Call on all employees to cooperate in dealing with the threats. Do they know of anything an employee of the company may have done that might motivate someone to make the threats? Will they report all threats they receive even if they appear minor? Can they collect information to help deal with the threat? These are all causes in which you can enlist the employees of your company.

☛ When consulting with the police, be able to show records of when the threats began and how they progressed. Also, have tapes of any threatening telephone calls if available.

An Accident at a Company Event

Imagine there's been an accident at your company's booth at a trade show. Some panels have fallen and a number of people have been injured. Here's what to do in such situations:

☛ Assemble as many employees as possible to go to the booth to help out with the cleaning up under the supervision of the appropriate person. Even if you had entrusted all aspects of the running of the booth to an agency, your company must take steps to show that it is acting responsibly.

☛ An upper management person must visit the injured in the hospital to show the company's sincerity.

☛ Employees should try to be helpful to the injured.

☛ The company can show its sincerity in contacting the homes and families of the injured.

☛ To assist the police in their inquiries, employees should collect as much information as possible about the accident.

☛ Whenever there is an accident at an event, it's necessary to consider whether to cancel or postpone the event itself or any other high-profile activities related to the event.

Preventing Problems

With so many events being held these days, it's only a matter of common sense to take out sufficient insurance for your participation in such activities. The most desirable type of policy should cover even the models or actors hired for demonstrations and other functions at the booth. It's also useful to identify the areas of responsibility of your agency, the company that builds the exhibit for you and the owner of the conference facility.

Gross Misconduct by an Employee

An employee uses company funds for his own purpose or becomes embroiled in a public scandal. Here's what to do:

☛ As a result of news coverage or police investigation of criminal acts by employees, companies are sometimes flooded with complaints.

Choose someone who can take charge of all aspects of dealing with the public in regard to this matter, so that there will be no contradictions in what is said by the company.

☛ At the same time, select a person who will handle telephone inquiries about the matter. There should be no inconsistencies between what the two say. On the phone, it will be all the more important for the person speaking for the company to be cheerful and extra polite.

☛ There will be many calls from reporters, so it will be very important to avoid creating confusion on the company's position. Also, employees need to be warned that they are not free to give their personal opinions to reporters or agree to requests for interviews.

☛ Depending on the nature of the problem and its size, it's wise to present a report to special customers and related companies. Write a memo explaining what the facts of the matter are, and what you are doing to deal with the situation. The report format is systematic and authoritative. It eliminates the problem of especially valued clients hearing different versions of what happened from different people in the company.

☛ At such times, try to stay calm and perform your daily tasks as you would have before the scandal. At a time when the public is paying close attention to your company, all employees should be very careful about how they act and what they say in public.

Trouble in the Office Affects Everyone

When rumors start going around the office that there are frequent thefts and it appears the one responsible is not from outside, the whole company can be shaken. To solve this problem, all employees have to pool their efforts to make sure thefts don't happen.

☛ Thieves target lockers and desk drawers on payday or the day after. Managers should tell their subordinates at morning meetings that money should not be left around the company.

☛ Each person should be careful about his or her own property. If there is a theft of property, the person who suffered the loss should not make a public scene over it, but should report it immediately to his or her boss.

☛ Do not speculate or gossip about who the thief might be.

☛ Letting outsiders know about the thefts will lower the public's confidence in the company. This is strictly forbidden. Depending on the circumstances, however, it may be necessary to report the problem to the police.

Sexual Harassment

One day, a woman quit on the spot when a male coworker stroked her hair and said it was pretty. While that simple act does not sound serious enough to have provoked the response, it seems that same male employee had been repeating the same action over and over for some time. The woman became neurotic about his unwanted attention.

While the one who does it may think nothing of it and call it a form of joking, for the woman who must bear with such aggressive behavior day in and day out it's emotionally painful.

Sexual harassment is really a kind of bullying behavior. If this bullying is to disappear from the workplace, it must do so naturally. Make sure the atmosphere of the office is one in which male and female coworkers show respect for each other.

Be conscious of the need to improve conditions for women in the workplace:

☛ A boss should treat the women in the office as talented personnel, not just extra hands to help out with men's work.

☛ Obscene conversation, newspapers, magazines, books and photographs don't belong in the office.

☛ Caution employees to be alert for this type of behavior at parties where there will be drinking, and encourage them to maintain a pleasant atmosphere.

3

CHAPTER 7

ENTERTAINING

> ☛ Don't let the client use a penny of his own money. Entertaining means giving as well as taking.
>
> ☛ It's old-fashioned to let the entertaining go on until late in the evening. Keep it to about two hours.
>
> ☛ Use about three minutes to mention the business reason for the meeting and then don't touch on it again.
>
> ☛ The most important thing is to avoid leaving a bad impression on the client. Also, don't let your hopes get too high.
>
> ☛ Play up the client and his or his company's achievements, while downplaying yourself. Asking for too much, being too pushy or too obsequious can be the cause of eventual failure.
>
> ☛ Be considerate of those serving you in restaurants or caddying on the golf course. It makes for a more pleasant atmosphere for all.
>
> ☛ Always be able to step back from things and judge how well the other person is satisfied with the entertainment.

Being a Bit Over-Attentive is Just About Right

Having a Drink Together Means Getting to Know One Another

Human psychology is a strange thing. Once you've patted your neighbor's dog on the head, you never seem to mind his barking. When you feel someone is not that different from you, you become willing to put up with a little more for his sake and even cover up failures to the extent possible. This is only natural, since

Unexpected Results from Indirect Entertaining

Busy people are often invited out and become tired of the continuous round of entertaining involved in business. For such people, it's sometimes wise to simply say thanks for all they have done for you and your company, and then, instead of inviting them out for a night of drinking, offer gift certificates to a restaurant they can take their family to or health club, pool or concert tickets. This is indirect entertaining.

Executives who don't get to see their families very often will make a point of using these gifts and will be very grateful. Indirect entertaining works in unexpected ways afterwards.

you have come to know him and accept him for what he is. We entertain people for the same reason.

When you want to have someone do business with you over a long period of time, you try to make up for hard feelings created in the process of determining a price or deadline for a project. This is when you should entertain.

Entertainment Oils the Wheels

A middle manager from a food processing company, Mr. M, has seen his fair share of entertaining: "When I get an invitation to go out with suppliers to get to know them better, even after we've place an order with them for some heavy industrial equipment, I know there's something going on. Ah-ha, I think to myself, they're taking me out in advance because they don't think they can make the deadline or maybe they expect a problem to come up. Even though I suspect something, I attend anyway, not letting on that I know anything about their motives. That's because I, too, want to get a sense of what's going on."

Don't expect someone who's entertaining you to tell you at that time that the company will probably miss the deadline. What most likely will be said is no more than the factory has been very busy, or that their employees are working very hard at the time.

Mr. M continues: "If I hear that there's going to be a missed deadline while I'm being entertained, the purpose of inviting me has been defeated. At the very least, the news becomes burdensome to me. But by attending such a party, I can hear a variety of other information I could not otherwise get in the office, and I can also get a feel for who the other person really is. This makes it easier to handle situations that may come up in the future."

As Mr. M's comments reveal, you have to use all your wits to make sure you transmit a message properly to your customer without making him feel burdened.

Different Ways to View It

☛ There is no such thing as a party simply to get to know each other better. There is always an objective, and transmitting that message skillfully through your relationship with the other person is what entertaining is all about.

☛ Using company funds for entertaining means that it is part of the company's business. When it is recognized that the entertainment is necessary, money is budgeted for it, and those doing the entertaining try to achieve the best results possible while staying within the budget. At all times, you must stay conscious of the cost/performance factor.

Don't Overdo It

For what reason you don't know, but you have been invited out for an evening of drinking, singing and entertaining, or the company that has invited you presses you to agree to something inappropriate. On the way home from either of these evenings, it's only natural that you feel unpleasant. If that is the result, both of these attempts to entertain have been failures. The secret to entertaining well is to practice moderation.

☛ The evening should begin with a short statement of the purpose of the party or meeting by someone from the company that extended the invitation. If you wait until later to make this statement or speech, the guests will not be able to relax, since they'll wonder when you're going to get around to it or what is going to be said.

☛ When there is someone from your company who is not well acquainted with the guests, by all means introduce them as soon as possible. Meeting so many different people, the guests will have trouble remembering all of the right names and titles. You, of course, should memorize all the clients' names and positions, and remember all the faces.

☛ The boss and subordinates attending should try to enhance the reputation and stature of the person who most often deals with the client.

☛ While it's good to show your human side in entertaining, try to keep your own views of life, your interests and other personal matters to yourself as much as possible. It's also dangerous to discuss company gossip, or criticize your company or boss. Talking about philosophy or politics or other subjects that require a good deal of thought shows poor taste. But if you stick to the talking about the weather and general comments about the economy, the conversation won't go anywhere. As the conversation moves from one subject to the other, try selecting topics from the day's newspaper that may be of mutual interest.

☛ Good listeners are good at entertaining. A guest will be more satisfied with a conversation if you let him speak and establish a rapport in this way. When ending such an evening, show appreciation for having your guest take the trouble to educate you so well about so many things on a night that was simply intended for his enjoyment.

Department store general affairs manager Mr. A., a strong believer in this way to express appreciation to customers, explains: "The customer to whom I gave such tickets and gift certificates really saved me once after that. He gave me the name of someone in the company to go to when a problem came up later. It really helped. Indirect entertaining's real charm is that it's so different from the usual entertainment such executives experience."

A Profile for Entertaining

YOU'RE NOT ON YOUR OWN
The premise of all business entertainment is that one company meets another through their representatives. It is conducted according to company rules, with company funds and according to rank within the company. In other words, it must be done entirely within the bounds that the company prescribes.

THE POSITION IS IMPORTANT
A common complaint in the business world runs as follows: "I wined and dined the head of that department for years and then yesterday his position was filled by a new person. Now I have to start all over again."

Nevertheless, the person can carry on his relationship with the former head of the department and keep him in his human network, but the relationship becomes a personal one.

A Ship with an Amateur Captain Will Sink if it Springs a Leak — Choose a Veteran

The guests included a top executive in their group and you could only produce a manager. On top of that, the place was so noisy that no one could hear the conversation. In short, it was an evening that it would have been better not to have been scheduled in the first place.

Selecting the Right People

There should be parity between the number of people, as well as their positions, from your side and the guests. It's good practice to send a list to the guests in advance showing who from your company will attend. At that point, you can start to fine tune the list of attendees on both sides. If you don't start feeling out the guests early about who should attend, schedules can not be made, the timing of the event will be delayed and the purpose of arranging the entertainment will be defeated.

Selecting the Right Place

When entertaining for a very important objective, visit the restaurant in advance to make sure it is acceptable and speak with the person in charge. Make sure that there are no other major parties or events scheduled there on the day you have chosen. Carefully scrutinize the place to make sure the guests will be favorably impressed with it. Whether it's a drinking place or a golf course, choose a place where you think your guest will be most comfortable. Take into account the guest's age and rank in the company.

Getting the Content Right

Whether you are deciding what will be served and at what time or choosing how you and your guests will play a certain golf course, it takes a lot of thought. To insure that you can accomplish the objective you have set within the limited amount of time, start planning early.

Typical Entertaining Can be Boring

The typical style of entertaining involves drinking after working hours. This can be effective in its own way, but things are changing. With younger people putting more emphasis on their personal lives and with so many business people commuting to new communities farther out in the suburbs, it's more thoughtful if you make sure that when you entertain guests, you limit the time to about two hours. But exercise your creativity with that two hours.

Mr. K, a manager in the general affairs department of a trading company, gives this advice: "Select a restaurant that's serving cuisine that people are talking about now. Then, for the next meeting, choose a place that has interesting architectural details or has a unique atmosphere. Varying the places you entertain in can make things more interesting. Also, if souvenirs or gifts of the restaurant's specialties are necessary, arrange for something seasonal to be given to your guests."

The same Mr. K keeps records of each time he entertains, and always tries to arrange something different for the next time he sees each person. His guests always look forward to being surprised at his choices for entertainment.

For those who are busy both night and day, the business lunch is recommended. If it's to thank someone for working so hard for you, inviting the person and his family to an evening at the theater and then dinner can be effective. You can also deepen your relationship much better with golf, fishing or a short trip together than you can with entertainment that involves drinking only.

THE ILLS OF ENTERTAINING

Always keep a close eye on entertaining from the aspect of cost and time management. Misusing entertainment expenses, extravagance and waste can eventually swallow up the business person.

When You're Both Busy, Make it Lunch

When it's difficult to find an evening when you and your guest are both free, rather than put it off, it's better to schedule a business lunch instead. Since everybody eats lunch anyway, it can be easier for the other person to agree to than an appointment in the evening. A business lunch should run about an hour and a half. Reserve a room in a mutually convenient restaurant. When it's impossible to get a private room, try to get a table that's away from the others and quieter.

☛ Order what your guest likes in advance. Arrive about 10 minutes before the appointed time and make the arrangements to have the food served when you think best. Then, wait for your guest in the lobby or reception area. Since the lunch hour is busy, it's polite to wait for him so that you can show him to your table.

☛ Outline briefly what you wanted to discuss before the food is served. Make sure that nothing is served until you finish what you have to say.

☛ In selecting the place, ask your guest's opinion when you think it's necessary. Also, avoid places frequented by your boss or

Otsukiai NOW

Common sense tells us entertaining that exceeds certain limits can create a variety of ills, including damaging the public's confidence in the company. The business world is taking a fresh look at the escalating costs of entertaining with an eye toward reducing expenses. This reevaluation of entertaining has two aspects:

- ***Frequency of entertaining, number of personnel required, the places chosen and the unit costs involved.***

- ***The use of chauffeured cars for entertainment purposes.***

people from related companies, since you probably won't feel as at ease in them.

☛ Above all, indulge the guest and make him feel important. If you suddenly overwhelm him with documents and start discussing all sorts of details related to work, he'll wonder why you didn't just ask to have a meeting at the office.

☛ Lunch is a good time to engage in more intellectual conversation. Choose topics that may be of interest to the guest. While relaxing, let your conversation expand.

Mr. H, a manager at a business machine manufacturer, thinks lunch can be very productive: "Usually, when you have lunch together, only a few people are involved and it doesn't take much preparation. You can talk about ideas or projects that would be more difficult to bring up in the more formal entertaining that takes place in the evening. It's an excellent way to get across a message in a relaxed and pleasant setting."

Lunch has not taken hold as a way to entertain in Japan, and it still has a fresh feeling to it. But since it doesn't involve plying the guest with alcohol, it's easy to see how people can enjoy it more and feel more relaxed about it. Depending on the time and the place, you can use lunches skillfully for entertaining your company's guests.

Enjoy Alcohol but Don't Overdo it

Entertaining is a Failure if It Ends in a Drunken Mess

Alcohol is man's friend. It relieves our sadness and makes our happiness seem all the more joyous. But it is a mistake to think that merely by having drinks with people you can have a successful relationship. On the other hand, alcohol does loosen our tongues and make us all a bit more talkative. That's all.

It's a failure if, under the influence of alcohol, you attempt to become too friendly with the guest. The guest may humor you and go along with it for awhile, but getting drunk and singing shoulder to shoulder will not give him a favorable impression of the company. Don't push the guest to drink a lot either. If he ends up with a hangover the next day, it's likely that he'll blame you for continuing to pour.

Everyone has a different approach to drinking. While asking about likes and dislikes and what he cares to drink, pay close attention to how the other person drinks. Adjust the pace of your consumption to his.

Considerations that Make for Success

☛ Eat a light snack around 4 p.m. so that you won't be drinking on an empty stomach.

☛ Make sure that pitchers of water or tea are placed next to older people and those who can't drink well. That way, they can stop drinking alcoholic beverages without anyone noticing.

☛ Treat the employees of the restaurant well. Don't go ordering them around and complaining about the service. It detracts from the atmosphere.

☛ Don't focus all your attention on just one person, no matter how important he or she is. The other people at the party will notice this and comment about it the following day.

☛ Inviting someone to a second nightspot after leaving the first will have an effect on a person's performance at work the next day. Don't argue too persuasively when you extend the invitation. If the guest is agreeable to continuing, don't go to a place you've never been to before and where your guest might possibly be offended by poor service or some other problem. Choose a place you know well and give the manager a call to make sure he will be able to provide what you and your guest want.

Restaurants

Ask the manager what other companies have reserved private rooms on the day you want. You don't want to run into a competitor in the hallway when you're entertaining a client. Also, make arrangements with the manager in advance for transportation and for wrapped gifts of the restaurant's specialties for the guests to take home.

Mr. H, a manager at an information processing company, offers a few hints for making sure the entertaining goes well: "Have the restaurant prepare several different brands of beer, since guests will usually have their preferences. Also, it's a good idea to put 2,000-3,000 yen in an envelope to give to the driver so that he can enjoy dinner somewhere while he waits for the party to come out of the restaurant. And finally, if you are the one being entertained, when offered the seat of honor at the table, it's appropriate to make as if you wish someone else to sit there. Do this twice and then accept this seat the third time it is offered to you.

Failures Happen

"On the day I was to meet my guest, an emergency came up so I missed having lunch. When I met him that evening and I began drinking on an empty stomach, the alcohol really hit me. This never happened before, but I became completely drunk and ruined the evening. Now that I think of it, the emergency that came up was nothing at all compared to the importance of properly entertaining such a prized customer. If you're too occupied with the things that are right in front of your eyes, you lose sight of what's important."

— Mr. A,
Insurance Company Executive

Otsukiai NOW

It's very expensive to pay for a car to take someone home in the evening after public transportation shuts down. Signs of change include:

- ***companies that require that entertaining end early enough for everyone to take public transportation home.***

- ***companies that forbid anyone from their purchasing departments or those charged with giving out construction contracts from accepting invitations for golf, evenings out on the town, etc, from supplier companies.***

This movement toward a reevaluation will become a plus for both the host and guest if it contributes to establishing a better framework in which both can improve their understanding of each other in a more natural, pleasant way.

Night Clubs and Bars

"You go to clubs to relax and not think about business, so be generous with the hostesses," advises Mr. K, the trading company executive mentioned earlier. "Instead of going to a place I know, I usually ask the guest what clubs he likes, and then we go to one of those. That way, there are never any problems."

Mr. K knows that if you go to a place that you frequent, the club's people will focus their attention on you instead of on your guest. In such cases, it's a good idea to make sure in advance that the check will be brought to you and not to your guest.

Karaoke Bars

Mr. T, a manager at a food processing company, gives this advice: "When you go to a singing pub, or karaoke bar, make sure that for every time you hold the mike, the guest holds it three times. There are times when the guest just can't sing or is shy about it, which makes things somewhat difficult. Others just want to sing and do nothing else. I fill the time between the guest's turn at the mike by discussing how to sing certain songs, songs that bring back different memories and other topics. I try to make the conversation humorous as well. Generally speaking, I like to take guests to places where there is a guitarist to accompany them while they sing. A good guitarist is easy to sing to and will cover up when your singing isn't very good."

If more than half of the guests you are entertaining don't like singing, don't go to a karaoke bar. It's wise to remember that there is an "anti-karaoke" element.

When You Are Being Entertained

☛ Whenever you are invited out, report it to your boss. When you feel that the entertainment is too lavish or that there's something else strange about it, talk it over with him.

☛ When you are invited out by a designated supplier before a contract is bid out, refuse the invitation. If you accept, you will be the object of suspicion from both within and outside the company.

☛ When your boss has been invited out, a subordinate or secretary from the other company may call to make arrangements. Feel free to let them know what your boss's preferences are in eating and whether or not he likes to drink. This can also be a good chance to extend your human network.

At the Restaurant

☛ If you and the other guests arrive earlier than the hosts, don't take seats. Often, there will be no clear idea of how to seat everyone until the entire party arrives.

☛ Just because you are the one being entertained, don't become arrogant. Don't ask to change the schedule or make impossible demands of your host. The evening was planned by them, so you should leave all details up to them.

☛ That said, if you are not feeling well or have to leave on a business trip the following morning, it's important to call the person on the host's side who is coordinating the party to let him know so that he can keep the party short. When you can tell that a party is going to run long, you can also arrange for an "emergency escape" from the proceedings. Just have someone call you at the restaurant and ask you to return to the office on an urgent business matter.

☛ If you attend a party with an overbearing boss, and you pay too much attention to him in the course of the evening, the people

Under the Cherry Trees

A client mentioned that he enjoyed watching the cherry blossoms, but could not find a quiet enough place. His supplier remembered a restaurant in the suburbs that was surrounded by cherry trees and invited him. Since then, it has become an annual event for the two and the amount of business between the two companies has steadily expanded.

Souvenirs from Entertaining

Often, as you leave after being entertained, you're handed a package to take home "for your children." Usually it's a cake or pastry, but by the time you arrive home, the children are already asleep and the cake has most likely been crushed. Undoubtedly, this leaves a bad impression. In selecting such souvenirs, choose:

☛ things that don't spoil or otherwise go bad;

☛ things that are not bulky or heavy;

☛ things that are considered rare or unusual and which the family will enjoy.

Most important is to prepare this present in advance. If you forget, probably the only thing available at the restaurant on such short notice will be some sort of cake.

Sometimes a Cup of Coffee is Enough

A quiet and very shy person, the manager of a client company, would always refuse to go out for entertaining because he could not tolerate alcohol. Mr. Y learned that he liked coffee, however, and asked him to join him for a cup at a special coffee house. The manager accepted the invitation and thoroughly enjoyed himself. Mr. Y now entertains the manager over lunch and always with a cup of delicious coffee.

from the host side will get the impression that you aren't a very substantial person.

☛ The day after being someone's guest, you should call to thank them. You can call those involved in setting up the party, and leave a message from your boss to their's thanking him for the evening. This becomes a thank-you to that entire company on behalf of everyone who was their guest the evening before.

The point is to create the feeling of a nice balance. Try to make sure that in the atmosphere, the flow of the proceedings and in what was said, the hosts and guests maintain this balance.

Various Ways to Entertain

Golf

A gentleman's sport, golf is a form of entertaining that is useful for exchanging information and engaging in a more natural type of communication. Those who are entertaining can enjoy the game while working at creating a pleasant atmosphere.

☛ It's generally accepted that the host will send a car to pick up a guest and will also have him driven home.

☛ For prizes, choose something the guest can take home to his family. Rather than something big and bulky, gift certificates are now the prize of choice.

☛ It's common practice to give the guest golf balls and tees before starting to play.

Trips

Taking a guest on a trip is a big responsibility, but it is very productive. There is nothing like viewing the open sky on a trip to open someone's heart.

Taking a trip with a guest calls for abundant consideration. The host must place the guest's safety above all else. Of course, you want the trip to be dramatic enough for them to remember and pleasant to recall in the future. But for safety's sake, take out travel insurance for them, make a list of family members you can contact in case of an emergency and check the availability of medical attention and facilities in the area in which you plan to travel.

To allow your guest to travel in comfort, let him know the weather conditions in the region. Don't make the schedule too detailed, and do your best to find good hotels and other places to stay.

Have a Half Day? Why Not Use It?

A guest has come on a business trip and has a half day left over before he's scheduled to return home. You've been assigned to show him around.

Here's what Mr. O, an executive of an industry organization suggests: "If you only have a half day, choose someplace that's convenient. If the guest likes art, you can suggest a museum. When you enter and buy his tickets, purchase pamphlets, a guide book and post card set that you can give him after you leave. This becomes a nice souvenir of the day. You can also try taking him to places that are in the news for whatever reason: areas that have been redeveloped for leisure use and other interesting destinations. Express your own sincerity to him by buying a small souvenir for about 1000 yen. He'll understand that this is from you and not the company, and will be touched by your generosity."

This type of entertaining is a great way to build your human network.

PART 4

CEREMONIES ARE THE PEAK FOR OTSUKIAI

DO YOUR BEST TO MAKE THEM SPECIAL

CHAPTER 1

COMMEMORATION CEREMONIES

The Whole Company Shows Its Gratitude

☛ When addressing invitations, use a writing brush to do the names and affix an attractive commemorative stamp.

☛ Mail out invitations so that they arrive 40 days before the ceremony.

☛ For a party on the completion of a new company facility, the building itself is the star attraction. Be sure to display a miniature model and photographs of the building.

☛ A ceremony on the inauguration of a new company president will attract the media. Don't give the appearance of extravagance.

☛ The ceremony should maintain an air of solemnity. Shinto rituals should be performed as directed by a Shinto priest.

☛ There will plenty of VIPs on hand at such ceremonies. Be careful about seating arrangements.

☛ Use your creativity in choosing a commemorative gift to give guests at the ceremony.

Ceremonies are Great PR Opportunities But Minute Preparation is What Makes the Difference

For the annual celebration of the founding of the company, you can handle all aspects of the ceremony within the company. But when it comes to the 20th or 30th anniversary, it's a different matter. The ceremony increases in scale. You have to bring together a special project team, and make very detailed preparations. What should you concentrate on in all this work? Ask someone in the company who has had the experience of working on similar events in the past.

Guests Appreciate the Small Details

How invitations are addressed depends on the rank of the person receiving them. For the highest-ranked people, the invitations should be addressed using a writing brush. Confirm the titles of those invited by phone and instead of ordinary postage use large and and very beautiful commemorative postage stamps. This increases the chances the person will open the letter and read it.

For those VIPs whose presence is vital to the ceremony, arrange to pay a visit at a specified time in advance of the day. Important people are usually very busy, so you'll need to get the event on their calendars as soon as possible. Also, talk to their secretaries and have them contact you should the person be called away on an emergency business trip that might prevent their attendance. Even if they're going to be unable to attend, you can ask for a comment that can be read at the ceremony or used at some other point in the proceedings.

Glass company executive Mr. C remembers a ceremony his company held not too long ago: "At the party after the ceremony, we had to have every brand of beer made in Japan for our guests to drink. The reason: we have two beer makers among our large clientele. If we had any less than every label on hand, it could possibly have offended either customer. It was a delicate matter."

Ceremonies Commemorating the Founding of the Company

Choose an auspicious day, according to the ancient Chinese calendar of taboo days. It should be during the work week, as close as possible to the actual anniversary, and the ceremony should

Ceremony Planning Flow

Decision on Date to Hold Ceremony	Target is a weekday and a "lucky day," according to the Chinese calendar.
Make a List of the Invitees	Affiliated companies, related government ministries. Classify by group.
▼	
Decide Content and Timing of Ceremony	
Project How Many Will Attend	At least 50% from any list will attend. For events with about 1000 guests, expect 60%. Attendance of 70% or more is considered an unqualified success.
▼	
Decide Site	Go over all necessary arrangements with a person in charge at the site (hotel, etc.).
Project Order of Ceremony Events	Assign necessary staff for each aspect of ceremony.
▼	
Decide Who's in Charge of What	
▼	
Order all Printed Materials	Proofread all materials scrupulously.
▼	
Make Charts of Order of Ceremonies	
Order Commemorative Gifts	
▼	
Confirm Those on Invitation Lists	
▼	
Check Progress of Each SectionWorking Ceremony	Escorts, reception, control of events, control of ceremony site and accounting.
Mail Invitations	Invitations should include information on the date and time, place, reason for the ceremony and whether business or formal attire is required. It must also ask if the guest will attend.
▼	
Confirm Budgets	
Preparation of Site, Food and Beverages, etc.	

start between 10 a.m. and 1 p.m. The ceremony and the party should take about two hours.

☛ Since so many guests have to be accommodated, most companies use hotels to hold such events. But if there is a large enough hall or other space within the company, it's better to hold the ceremony on the premises because you can show guests around your facilities.

☛ Prepare a list of guests and send out invitations 40 days before the day of the ceremony. Along with the invitation, you should enclose a stamped reply card, a map showing how to get to the ceremony site, and a ticket that can be exchanged for a gift at the ceremony. If there are parking facilities, enclose a ticket that will permit free parking for that day.

☛ For important customers, it is proper to hand deliver the invitation and request their attendance in person.

☛ At the site of the ceremony, display panels showing the progress of the company as well as company statistics and other information to convey to the guests the meaning of the ceremony and the company's happiness at this event. At the ceremony itself, it is also useful to show a video or slide presentation illustrating the company's history.

Ribbon-Cutting Ceremonies

☛ Prepare red and white ribbons.

☛ Those cutting the ribbon should be wearing formal attire and white gloves.

☛ The master of ceremonies introduces each of the dignitaries who will cut the ribbon.

☛ The master of ceremonies gives a signal to the cutters, and they all cut together.

☛ The order of seating is as follows: the main guest is at the center of the dais, the next most important on his right, the next on his left, and so on with the right preceding the left.

☛ The scissors should be extra-large, have a ribbon attached and be placed on a special tray.

☛ There should be two assistants stationed next to the dignitaries cutting the ribbon. As soon as the cut is made, they will take the scissors from the dignitaries and dispose of the ribbon.

☛ Consider the benefits of decorations and music.

☛ Have at least two photographers on hand to capture the event.

☛ At the party following the ceremony, it adds interest to announce new products or display various product exhibits. A new twist in marking such milestone events is to announce that a certain amount of money that would have been spent on the ceremony has instead been given to charity. Each guest is then given a certificate attesting to this as well as a small memento or gift to commemorate the anniversary.

Ceremonies for New Facilities

☛ A building completion ceremony is held to thank the Shinto gods for permitting the building to be erected without mishaps and to ask for divine protection in the future. If you ask, the construction company that erected your building can arrange this for you very easily. The ceremony itself should follow the directions laid down by the Shinto priest you engage for this purpose.

☛ The ribbon-cutting should be done by the president and the guests of honor.

☛ Show the guests of honor to the main area of the building.

☛ At the ceremony, there should be a few words from the president apologizing for the inconvenience created during the construction process and thanking everyone for their cooperation and support.

☛ For the benefit of the guests who are unable to arrive in time for the ceremony and only come to the party, prepare panels or display a miniature model of the new facility at the party site. Also be sure to distribute pamphlets and other company publications.

☛ It's wise to prepare an attraction related to the event for the pleasure of the guests: the singing of a lumber-carrier's chant or other such entertainment is a good choice.

Inauguration of a New President

Most often, the ceremony is held within the company for employees only, but the reception is held at a site outside the company later. The inauguaration ceremony is a great chance for the new president to announce his policies and principles and raise employee morale in particular. All of the company's top executives should publicly show their support for the president. It's also a good idea to show the list of invitees to the new president for his approval. It won't hurt to run the list by the departing president, either.

☛ It's natural to want to make the reception as elegant and refined as possible, but it's a good idea not to use too much money for this purpose. If the ceremony and party are viewed as extravagant by the guests, your company's fiscal health may be called into question.

☛ If employees cling together in groups and exchange whispered conversations with each other, guests will have doubts about the company's employee training policies and the company's structure. On this day, above all else, employees should be focused on pleasing the company's customers who are attending the events.

☛ Every employee should read and remember the new president's biography so they will be able to answer questions about him if asked by guests.

☛ For mementos marking the day, it's good practice not to give an extravagant gift. Present each guest with a product made by the company.

After the Ceremony

☛ Be prompt about sending thank-you's to important guests and those who made speeches at the event. It's also good manners to send a note of thanks to the master of ceremonies and the staff involved in the entertainment or other matters related to the ceremony.

☛ For those people who were unable to come to the ceremony, the memento or commemorative gift should be sent along with a note asking for their good will in the future.

☛ The ceremony marks the start of a new era for a company. After the ceremony is over, however, you can still publicize its significance. For example, you can have snapshots of the event framed in holders and given to key figures. Also, if the press carries interviews of the new president, get copies of the articles and distribute them to get more mileage out of the event. All such measures deepen the impact of the event.

CHAPTER 2

IN-COMPANY EVENTS

Enjoy Seeing Everyone's True Face

☛ Announce plans in each section on the first day back from the long New Year's Holiday. Stir people up.

☛ Whether it's a promotion or not, plan a farewell party whenever someone is going to be sent to another section.

☛ When you hold parties for new employees, be sensitive. Remember how you wished to be treated when you were new on the job.

☛ Company trips that involve drinking and gambling are old-fashioned. Plan events with a fresh, happy feeling.

☛ When drinking, don't forget your place. You are part of the company.

☛ Use prizes or certificates to create a lively, competitive atmosphere.

Participating and Cooperating in Events are Good Manners for the Business Person

Junior executive Mr. Y has worked at a computer company for three years. Here's why he thinks company events are important: "When I was a new employee, I felt that in-company events were only a bother and I really hated to be involved in them.

That continued until, at one company athletic event, I was paired in a three-legged race with a boss I was really afraid of. We came in last, and he came up to me later and apologized for having made us lose. After that I was able to talk to him without being afraid. The more I attended company events, the more comfortable I became in the company."

Company events are one link in the operation of a modern corporation. Each has its own special significance. By attending and participating in them, you play a part in how the company is run.

All Kinds of Events

Starting the Year Ceremonies

☛ On the first day back to work after the New Year's holidays, everyone from the president on down assembles to pledge to each other that they will do their utmost for the company in that year. It's important to show a clear vision of the future and to stimulate morale. Also, in each department, managers should concisely announce their plans for the year.

☛ In most offices, the New Year ceremonies take about an hour in the morning. Depending on other circumstances, ceremonies are sometimes held later in the afternoon or after work. Refreshments are nothing more elaborate than beer and some light snacks.

☛ To mark the first shipment of the year, assemble all employees at the entrance of the building to applaud as they see off the products.

☛ The number of women who come to the office dressed in kimono on the first day of work is on the decline nowadays. Since each company has different policies, it's better to inquire ahead of time about what to do.

Ceremonies for New Employees Entering the Company

☛ Ordinarily, ceremonies to induct new employees are held in a hall or conference room at the company. But for companies that have a great many new employees, a hall outside the company is sometimes rented.

☛ As soon as the time and place are settled, send out notices to the relevant sections.

☛ Let the new employees know that everyone in the company is looking forward to welcoming them. Every member of the top management team, not just the president, should give an effective speech, expressing the hopes they are placing in the new employees. Again, Mr. Y gives his thoughts: "When I received my invitation to the ceremony welcoming that year's new employees to the company, I was encouraged by a message from the president. I felt I had to do my best for the company. Then, on the day of the ceremony, as we entered the hall, we were greeted by the welcoming applause of everyone in the company. At the end of the ceremony, the president shook hands with each of us. It was a very moving ceremony."

This is the only time in employees' lives that there will be a ceremony welcoming them into the company. Make sure it's one to remember.

Welcome Parties/Farewell Parties

☛ These are held on the department or section level. It's best to follow the practice of the particular section in deciding the type of party.

☛ When parties are held to simultaneously bid farewell to someone who is being transferred or is retiring and to welcome his replacement, the person who is leaving should take precedence in all aspects of the ceremony.

☛ Managers who are being transferred react differently depending on the reason or type of transfer. It could be a promotion, or it might well be an unaccompanied assignment to a distant part of

Events to Spark Motivation

Speech Contests and Announcements of Company Study Circle Results

Teams or individuals can announce the results of their studies. Presentations can be judged and certificates awarded to those with the best results.

Art Exhibits

Exhibiting the paintings, calligraphy and other artwork done by employees outside of work lets employees show off their interests and skills.

For design studios and advertising agencies, such events can be a good opportunity to publicize themselves.

Cherry-Blossom/Plum-Blossom Viewing

The flowering of cherry and plum trees early in spring presents the opportunity to improve communication in a natural setting outside the company and away from the small drinking places usually chosen for this purpose.

the country or overseas. It might also be retirement. If there seems to be some unwillingness to have a party on the part of the person leaving, ask the person in the section with whom he was closest to arrange the party. Also, at the party be sure to make speeches that praise his strong points.

☛ When someone is being transferred to your section from another part of the company, take care in introducing him at his welcome party. First, make sure you correctly describe where he worked before and what the nature of his work will be. This will make it easier for everyone to talk to him. You should also try to avoid subjecting him to a shower of questions as he's being introduced. That's okay in a one-on-one situation, but it's not appropriate when one person has to meet a group of people.

Recreation is a Chance to Strengthen Your Human Network

Employee Trips

Mr. S, a manager of a textile company, explains how he handled employee trips when he was put in charge of the project one year:

"I used my wordprocessor to make a little booklet on the destination of our trip, and then I had it distributed to all employees. It contained information on interesting places around the site we were to visit, notes on the local cuisine, local brands of saké and the benefits of bathing in the local hot springs, as well as several maps. It made a big hit. Everyone loved it and carried it along wherever they went on the trip."

If you're put in charge of handling such trips, your toughest problems will be assigning rooms and coming up with interesting ways for the group to spend the day together. Here are some hints to start with:

☛ In the assigning of rooms, it's best to start by asking the higher management what rooms they would like. After hearing their preferences you, as coordinator, can assign rooms to all others as you think best. As a general rule, it's best to assign people who do not work together at the office to room together.

☛ However, it's a good idea to group certain types of people together: those who will like to drink heavily, those who wish to play golf in the morning, mahjong players, etc. Also, have separate rooms for those who have no trouble sleeping and those who snore. Everyone will thank you.

☛ Your room should be in the middle of the others, or in some location where everyone can easily contact you should they need to.

☛ For activities, don't limit things to tennis and golf. Make arrangements for hiking, sightseeing and other activities that non-athletes can enjoy as part of the agenda.

☛ Those who participate in these trips should try not to limit their activities to those they usually associate with at work. Everyone should try to be considerate and make sure that no one is left out of the fun.

Year-End Parties

In planning year-end parties, 70% of the success of the event will come from reserving the right place well enough in advance. Start looking for a site in November.

Recently, we see more year-end parties at which the participants stay overnight at the hotel or inn where the party is held. One advantage is that it's relatively inexpensive. Also, since there's no late-night commute back home, it's easier the next day and you can get to know people at a more leisurely pace. Reservations for such places should be made at the start of fall.

Keep in mind these considerations for year-end parties:

☛ Plan to end the party by 9 p.m. out of consideration for those who have long commutes back home.

☛ The coordinator of the party should send all participants a short memo, giving the time and place for the party and instructions on how to get there. The coordinator should also ask the president to make a speech and the vice president to lead a round of toasts.

☛ The place should be spacious. Things will become uncomfortable if people are stuck sitting in one place and cannot move around.

☛ Decide on entertainment or attractions that everyone can enjoy. Drawings for prizes and bingo are reliable favorites.

☛ Have an "appropriate" amount of food and beverages. If people drink too much they become boisterous and start bickering. Keep an eye on things.

☛ This is a once-a-year event. Don't let alcohol cause any

breaches in decorum.

☛ Male employees should help out with the proceedings to make things go smoother. Ordering female employees about and asking them to serve you is out.

Other Company Events

Awards Programs

☛ To recognize and encourage achievement, present certificates, money, models etc. in company ceremonies.

☛ Recipients of awards should dress simply and prepare a short speech of appreciation.

Determination Ceremonies

☛ Ceremonies to express a sense of determination are held when a number of people from the company will be sent to represent the company in outside training, on study tours overseas or in tournaments or other contests. These ceremonies are held during the lunch break or after work. Ceremonies are not held during regular working hours out of consideration for other employees.

Athletic Events, Hikes, etc.

☛ There are events that involve the whole company and events that only involve those who organize and run them. In either case, be an active participant.

☛ Each year, a company will sponsor an outdoor athletic meet for all employees. For busy people who don't get much chance to exercise, these events are a great way to work off stress. Making one section or department compete against another is a good way to encourage competitiveness and interest in the events. People will enjoy relay races, parades of the contesting teams and other such features.

☛ Company hikes should be scheduled on a course that's not too difficult and led by an experienced hiker. It's good trail manners not to leave any refuse behind, and to give a friendly greeting to any hikers you meet coming from the opposite direction.

CHAPTER 3

PARTIES

Here's Where You See What the Company is Really about

- ☛ Through your routine information collection activities, you'll know who to invite.
- ☛ Expect about half of those invited to attend.
- ☛ You'll need more food for parties at which there are many female guests. Take this into account when budgeting.
- ☛ Make sure there is enough room for guests to be comfortable. A good rule is 2.5 people per *tsubo* (about 4 sq. yds.).
- ☛ The person handling the receiving of guests should have receipts handy (if a party fee is collected).
- ☛ Place the most popular dishes away from where the flow of party traffic is poor.

The Secret to a Good Party is How You Orchestrate It

Consideration is More Important than Money

We use the word "party" to describe a variety of events, everything from large-scale ceremonies and receptions to small get-togethers. But for all these events, the common factor in success is good preparation. Keep in mind that preparation is 80% of the event, and the other 20% is whatever you do on the day of the event.

The Invitation List Determines the Fate of the Party

You have to start by asking yourself how many people you want to bring together for the party. Once you do that, you can select a place for it and decide whether it will be a sit-down affair or a buffet-style party. More importantly, you can start drawing up a budget for it. So you should put priority on making a good list of people to invite.

Since each of the departments dealing with customers and others outside the company will have the best information for your purposes, consult with the appropriate people from each of them. Make the list, incorporating their suggestions.

Calculate the Budget Based on the Invitation List

Mr. M, a manager at an electronics manufacturer, gives this advice in planning a budget for your party: "If you invite 200 people, count on about half, or 100, coming. If the party is going to be a sit-down affair, multiply the number of people by the cost per person for the type of food you'll be serving. If it's a buffet, you can multiply the cost per person by .7 times the number of people who'll be attending. However, if there are a lot of women among the invited guests, budget a little bit more. Women will gravitate toward the food rather than the alcohol at such events."

How much should you budget for drinks then? You can get 18-20 mixed drinks from a bottle of whiskey. At a usual party, someone in his thirties is likely to drink about 3.5 drinks. Someone older, say, in his fifties, will probably only consume three drinks. So for your average party, assume that each person will consume 3.3 drinks. For 100 people, that means 330 drinks will be needed, so you had better plan on having at least 18 bottles of whiskey on hand.

Parties also require other expenses, including the cost of flowers for each table, microphones, recording costs as well as the cost of entertainment—performers and hostesses.

Tricks to Boost Attendance

☛ Have a celebrity or other famous person sponsor the party. Don't just use his name, have him attend.

☛ Make your invitations intriguing. Use humor or some other creative device to interest people and make them attend. Pay attention to the design especially.

☛ Have a skilled calligrapher do the addressing of the invitations with a writing brush. Invitations written in a sloppy hand in either ballpoint or fountain pen will detract from attendance.

☛ For special guests, sending an invitation is not sufficient. Visit or at least telephone them to request their attendance.

☛ Depending on the type of party you're having, you can also invite the media and get some publicity value from it.

Pay Attention to the Flow of People

Choosing the Wrong Place Can Be a Tragedy

"As soon as you stepped into the place, you couldn't move. The place was so packed that I couldn't reach the food. Not enough tables, no way to get to the food and I was really famished. That party made me so angry." Such complaints are by no means unusual. They are the result of mistakes by the host in selecting the place for the party. For a good flow of people and a feeling of

Good Partygivers Can Predict the Flow of Party Traffic

People enter from the rear of the hall, pass through D zone and congregate in C zone. Very few go to B zone and almost none to A zone.

Place popular food stations, like sushi and tempura, in A zone to lure party guests into that area.

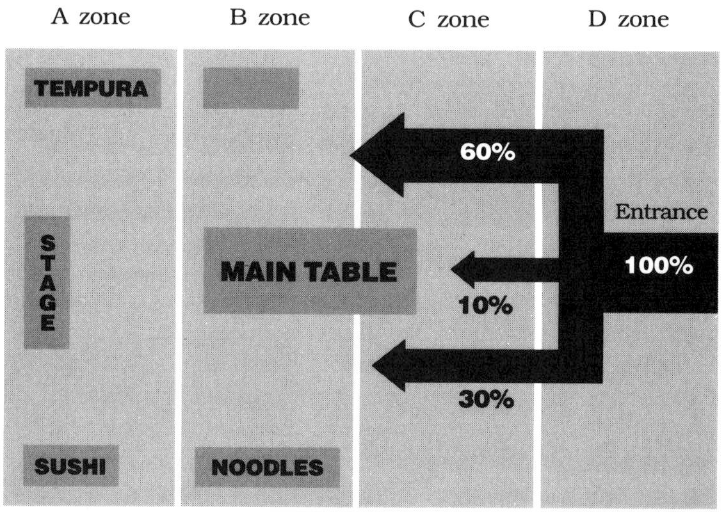

spaciousness, allow one *tsubo* (about 4 sq. yards) for each 2.5 to 3 people. Project how many people will attend and then select the place for the party.

☛ Check to make sure there are adequate rooms for the main guest, the hosts and entertainers (if hired). If the cloak room and the reception are far apart, set up a temporary cloak room nearby.

Change the Flow of People by Using Food

It reflects badly on the company when food is served at a buffet and disappears in short order. On the other hand, if food is left over, it seems embarrassing and the hosts wonder if it tasted all right. Party food gives you the chance to raise your company in the eyes of those who don't expect anything very tasty at a party.

☛ One veteran host explains his strategy for placing food at parties, using the illustration below: "At parties, people tend to collect in a particular area. Of those who enter the hall, most will go through the D zone and find a comfortable spot in the C zone. Very few will venture into the B zone and almost none into the A zone. For this reason, we place the very popular tempura and sushi stations in this area. By doing so, you bring more people into the A zone and even out the density of the population inside the hall."

You Can Tell a Lot about the Quality of the Party by Looking at the Reception Desk

Those in charge of the reception area determine the impression the guest will have from the party. Guests' name badges should be arranged in alphabetical order on the reception tables. Guests should not be kept waiting to be checked into the party.

The most frequently asked question at the reception desks are the following:

☛ "Where are the rest rooms?"

☛ "Where are the telephones?" and

☛ "Where is the cloakroom?

You should decide in advance how you can most efficiently explain to guests the location for each of them. Also, have on hand a good supply of change to give to guests for telephone calls.

Otsukiai Today

For today's busy executive, the typical party is regarded as a waste of time, money and energy. To counter this attitude, there is a gradual shift away from the large-scale parties of the past that featured lavish entertainment, expensive decorations and tables piled with food. Today we see more smaller parties held for employees of one section of the company in which the aim is to deepen friendships of the group. There are also more parties in which all who attend have a clear understanding of the purpose of the event. For example, guests from various affiliated companies will be invited to hear a lecture for their edification and then to join in a party afterwards. There are also cases in which new product announcements or product monitoring are combined with a party. Parties that offer a newsworthy angle and economical considerations are also on the rise.

Pointers for Making a Lively Party

☛ The emcee, as a representative of the hosts at the party, plays a very key role as the moodmaker. Choose someone who can play the role modestly and well. But remember that someone who is too enthusiastic can leave a poor impression. When an amateur is to be the emcee, he or she should aim for accuracy rather than try to create a warm reception from the audience. When someone from outside the company is chosen to do the job of master of ceremonies, usually a professional speaker, be sure that he studies about the company in advance. A lecture on the company should be arranged for him and he should be fully briefed on all the events of the day.

When introducing those who will speak, be especially careful to give their proper full names and titles. Add "san" or "sama" for business people, and "sensei" for doctors, educators and the like.

☛ Do your best to provide interesting entertainment for the party. Sometimes it seems that people who plan parties play it safe and choose the same sort of music. Be resourceful and find interesting traditional music, or music that is played on unusual instruments. At the party following a formal ceremony, have an employee band play for everyone's enjoyment.

CHAPTER 4

FOREIGNERS

- ☛ Don't bow as you shake hands. Meaningless laughing is also on the list of taboos.
- ☛ When you're really worried about how well you'll be able to speak with foreigners, use an interpreter.
- ☛ Remember the other person's name and use it when you speak with them.
- ☛ Be aware of differences in culture and customs. Forcing people to eat what you like will make them dislike you.
- ☛ Foreigners who are not familiar with the local geography should not be seen out and left to their own resources. Also, for important meetings, send someone to pick up your foreign guests.
- ☛ Invite their wives to parties. Have your executives' spouses attend also.
- ☛ Always specify on printed invitations how they should dress.

It's Not Your Ability in Languages, it's How You Deal with People

Don't Be Too Excited and Don't Worry — Stay Cool

It's a strange spectacle but one we often see nonetheless. The Japanese who is introduced to the foreigner greets him in his own language but bows continuously. There are even some who manage to utter a greeting, shake hands and bow simultaneously.

When you meet someone, you should smile, meet his or her eyes and give a firm handshake. Even if you can't speak foreign languages, being able to do this will give you the air of an internationally oriented person. Just because the other person is a foreigner, there's no reason to become overexcited or anxious about meeting him. Stay calm, rid yourself of the idea that you

Be Sensitive about Foreign Dietary Habits

After casually asking a foreign customer if he'd like to have a drink, more than one person has been surprised to get an angry "No" in response. Islam forbids all Muslims from partaking in alcoholic beverages. Being ignorant of the customs of foreign countries can result in embarrassment for you and your company. Keep in mind that Hinduism prohibits the consumption of beef and Judaism forbids the eating of pork, squid, octopus, shrimp and crabs.

can't deal with foreigners and set your sights on becoming more international.

Use Interpreters Often

Mr. F, a manager at a steelmaking company, has had much experience in negotiating with foreigners. Here's what he advises: "I was talking with a foreign customer when I realized I wasn't following what he was saying. In any case, I thought, 'It doesn't make much difference,' so I just kept nodding. All of a sudden he just blew up at me. Ever since that experience, I always call in an interpreter whenever I'm not confident I can handle the language in a deal with foreigners."

In dealings with foreigners, don't use ambiguous expressions which can mislead the other person, and be careful to avoid meaningless laughter. In major business dealings, little things like these can lead to failure.

☛ When foreigners will be present at a business meeting, prepare translations of all materials in advance. If it's possible, there should be an interpreter for you and the foreigner. In particular, when meeting with Americans and Europeans who come from countries where the anti-smoking movement has taken strong hold, send a note around to your colleagues asking them to refrain from smoking. As an alternative, reserve a room for the meeting that is equipped with an air cleaning device.

Show extra consideration for the visitor by going to his hotel to meet him on the day of the meeting. Mr. F adds: "In the past, foreign visitors have turned up late for meetings because they weren't aware of how to ride our trains. For those who are visiting Japan for the first time, it's especially important to give detailed advice on shopping, meals and other aspects of life in this country."

First Names Bring People Closer

After exchanging business cards, take note of the other person's first name and use it aggressively in your conversation to achieve a feeling of closeness. Also, in introducing people or being introduced, stand at attention. If the other person is more senior or older, he should make the move to shake hands.

CHAPTER 5

MAKING SPEECHES

- ☛ The speed at which you speak should stay between 160 and 180 words a minute.
- ☛ Flamboyant gestures invite disaster. Hold back on the performing.
- ☛ Keep your speeches short, sensible and crisp.
- ☛ In farewell speeches, touch on the person's warm human nature and congratulate him on his future undertaking.
- ☛ Speeches at year-end parties should not be too formal. Keep them upbeat.
- ☛ There is no such thing as an innate talent for speaking. Practice makes a good speaker.
- ☛ Your speeches have the right stuff if they evoke a reaction from your listeners.

Leave Them Feeling Warm All Over

A Poor Talker Isn't Necessarily a Poor Speaker

Whether it's in a business meeting in the company or an event outside, or even a social event, there is no separating the life of a business person from the making of speeches. Don't think that because you're a poor talker you'll be a poor speaker. There are simple tricks you can learn in order to become a good speaker.

Seven Rules for Speech Making

Mr. Y lectures housewives on the art of speaking, and has a comprehensive approach to making the best of a speaking opportunity: "Speaking is a type of performance. It's not just the words you say, it's the expression on your face, how you move your hands and how you establish eye contact with the audience."

Here are his seven rules for effective speech making:

Rule 1: Speak more slowly than you usually do. There are about 200 words on the average manuscript page used for writing speeches. The speaker should cover 160-180 words a minute, in other words a little less than a page.

Rule 2: The first 10 seconds are the trick. To get the audience's attention, you should avoid the ordinary worn-out greetings. Why not start by relating something that happened to you that day that might be of interest to your listeners?

Rule 3: Learn the effective use of pauses. Listeners will hang on your words if you do.

Rule 4: Look directly at your audience. It's rude to look up or off to the side and it also prevents your feelings from being communicated properly. Don't focus on one person in the audience, either. It may help you concentrate, but it will be difficult for the person who is being singled out for your attention.

Rule 5: Be expressive. Use gestures appropriately, but don't overdo it. Japanese audiences don't warm up to excessively theatrical gestures.

Rule 6: Use a concrete, easy-to-understand quote to perk up interest. Select your words carefully to evoke a scene in the mind of each listener.

Rule 7: Use humorous or witty anecdotes. The speech should be short, sensible and crisp.

Everyone Gets Nervous — Stay Calm and Go Slowly

Keep in mind that everyone gets nervous before making a speech, so start off slowly and allow yourself the time to become confident. Also, don't use stories or anecdotes borrowed from others because once you get nervous you can forget the details very easily. Speak from your own experience in your own way.

Speeches for Every Purpose

At In-Company Business Meetings

First, thank everyone for sparing the time from their busy schedules to get together for the meeting, and then concisely describe the purpose of the meeting.

In preparing to speak at such meetings, remember to put emphasis into the part where you wrap up your introductory remarks. For example: "The implementation of this plan will show the level of our teamwork to those within and outside the company. At this meeting, let's establish a strong foundation on which we can build."

With such a strong call to action, you raise the sense of significance of the meeting and get the participants to more actively debate different positions.

At Outside Business Meetings

Put special emphasis on thanking everyone very politely for attending. Then describe the purpose of the meeting and why you have asked everyone to participate. In explaining the reason for the meeting, even if it's to discuss a problem, phrase it as a request for cooperation in dealing with such difficulties. This will make it easier for the other side to talk freely. Then briefly summarize the agenda of the meeting. If each participant has a clear picture in his head of what the order of business is, things will proceed more smoothly.

At Personnel Changes

When reassigned, you'll be asked to introduce yourself formally to your new section. Give your title and name clearly, explain what you did in your previous job and what responsibilities you will have in your new position. Avoid any hint of boastfulness.

For example, don't brag about keeping your previous department in its number one sales position within the company or having achieved a high level of proficiency in the English language or being a master of kendo. Even if it's true, be modest about such accomplishments in your introductory speech.

Also, don't say too much about your hobbies or interests. Announcing to everyone that you like playing tennis and enjoy writing haiku may irritate those who work hard and don't have time for such hobbies.

Learn from Kabuki Actors

On the hanamichi (the long auxiliary stage that runs from the back of the theater up to the main stage) the Kabuki actor strikes poses three times: to the left, to the center and then to the right. He does this to please everyone in the audience equally. No matter how large the hall, if you follow the same procedure, shifting your view from the left to the center and then to the right, everyone present will feel that you are speaking directly to them. This also solves the problem of where you should focus your eyes when speaking.

Thoughts to Keep from Getting Nervous

- ***Everyone is nervous about making speeches. It's not just you.***
- ***No one is really listening that closely anyway.***
- ***Right. This is a great topic. They'll love it.***
- ***The audience is full of blockheads anyway.***
- ***There are some very important people listening, but we're all the same under our clothes.***
- ***I am a genius. I am a genius. I am a genius.***

In closing, it's wise to say something along this line to ask for everyone's cooperation and help: "I hope that, as time passes, you will all think of me as someone you can rely on. I would appreciate anything you can do to help me reach that point. Thank you very much."

At Farewells

Partings are by nature sad affairs, but you can brighten them up by congratulating the person on his new status and wishing him a bright future. In recalling the person's career, be sure to mention things that show him in a positive light, and speak of how his personality and other characteristics will be valuable to him in his new position.

When the departing person is leaving against his will or is resigning or retiring, stress his humanity in your remarks, and close by expressing your wishes for his future growth and success.

You, Too, Can Be a Good Speaker

Mr. S, a manager at a trading company, tells how he improved as a speaker: "Together with four colleagues from work, I started a speech club. The impetus for doing this was my anxiety over having to give a short speech at a business event. We started with speeches in Japanese, which we gave once a week at a different member's house.

"We would write a noun, like "desk" or "word processor" on index cards and then turn them over. Each member would then pick a card and speak extemporaneously on that subject. This opportunity to play with words and use our imagination was very valuable. One technique we used to come up with thoughts on any subject was to add the word "my" before the noun. Speaking about "my desk" or "my music" was easy and a lot of fun.

"By repeating this exercise over and over, we all became good speakers. It wasn't long before we were able to stand up and speak confidently whenever we were asked to say a few words at business events. You can also use this same technique to develop your ability to speak before foreign audiences."

CHAPTER 6

GIFTS

☛ Expensive gifts in the gift-giving season become a burden on the receiver.

☛ For someone who is on an unaccompanied assignment, send gifts directly to the family.

☛ When you wish to send a gift to someone and want to find out their address, don't ask in such a way that your purpose is clear. Find another way to do it.

☛ Send a thank-you as soon as you receive the gift. If you receive a gift from someone you don't want one from, not sending a thank-you note is the best way to express your feelings.

☛ Gifts delivered to the office, even if addressed to you personally, should be opened there. Taking them home looks greedy.

☛ Make a record of all the gifts you receive and don't forget where you leave it.

☛ If you make a contribution to a ceremony or other public undertaking, the recipient might make an announcement about it.

Gifts that Express Your Feelings

Be Smart about Gift Giving

Consider the Other Person's Position

Leasing company executive Mr. K discusses gift giving: "Giving someone a very valuable gift in either the summer or year-end gift-giving seasons places a burden on them. On the other hand, something of appropriate value that was selected especially for the recipient and expresses that feeling will make the person happy."

Summer and year-end gifts say "thank you for all you've done for me over the past season." The value of the gift should be in line with what is generally thought to be appropriate for that purpose, so that it will be welcomed by the recipient without any feelings of reservation. Additionally, you'll want to select gifts that take into consideration the other person's likes and dislikes and his position. You should also give thought to whether the gift is to be delivered to the person's office or home.

For Those on Unaccompanied Assignments

Sending a gift to the home of someone who is on an unaccompanied assignment in another part of the country is guaranteed to delight him. In fact, doing so is doubly effective. The gift will be more conspicuous because, while he's away, only about half as many gifts as in a usual year will be delivered to his home, and his family will make a long-distance call to him to tell him it has arrived.

When sending a gift directly to someone who is stationed away from his family, send confections or packages of fruit that can be easily divided for sharing with others. Whenever a gift is delivered to a company dormitory, it's not long before everyone knows about it. Under such circumstances, it's only human nature to want to share one's good fortune with others.

Keep a File of Home Addresses

Bank manager Mr. M sends gifts to the homes of people who have been especially helpful to him during the year, but getting home addresses is no easy chore: "I usually call the personnel department of the other person's company and say that I want to send a greeting card to him but don't know the right address. After they give me the address, I file it. I also file all copies of the shipping advice from each department store from which I have gifts sent. These show the proper address of each person. That way, all I have to do the following year is to confirm that the address is correct."

Keep Records of What You Send

It's a good idea to continue to send the same gifts. Consistently sending a gift of tea in one season and fruit in another leaves a deeper impression on the recipient of the gifts.

Attach a Hand-Written Card

Even when sending gifts directly from department stores, you create a better impression by attaching a hand-written greeting. It's a good idea to write out such cards well in advance and then insert them each time you buy a gift and are about to have the store send it.

Unwelcome Gifts

If you receive a gift from someone you don't like, accept it but then send him a gift worth exactly twice as much money as he spent. This is similar to the custom used in breaking off wedding engagements, and indicates to the other person that you wish to sever the relationship.

Good Timing is Everything

It's Okay to Ask the Person's Preferences

For mid-summer and year-end gifts for clients, visit the person's office and present them in person. Since this is a good opportunity to polish the image of your company, use great care in the selection of gifts for such purposes.

Occasions for Gifts

When Affiliated Companies Send Gifts to the Parent Company

Sending an extremely valuable gift will be taken as a sign of presumptuousness. Think of the content of the gift first, not the value. Perhaps the best gifts are beer, sake, coffee, confections and other consumable items that can be enjoyed by the parent company's employees at work or at work-related events.

For Hospital Visits

Ask when would be a convenient time before planning a visit. In the hospital room, be especially considerate and don't discuss the person's condition or his job, and don't stay too long.

OTSUKIAI TODAY

For some, mid-summer and year-end gift giving are the prime examples of socially approved but empty formalities that should be eliminated. In fact, there are some companies that forbid their employees to either give or receive such gifts. Other companies don't give the traditional summer gifts, but do send gifts at year's end, while others just send greeting cards and no gifts. One company based in the tea-growing prefecture of Shizuoka sends its customers a canister of newly picked tea at the height of that season, but sends no other gifts during the year. If a company sends around a notice of its intention not to engage in gift exchanges to all the companies it deals with, and they all agree to take similar measures, everyone can enjoy a more natural relationship and save money at the same time.

When you can't visit the hospital, send an appropriate greeting card and gift to the person's home. There are certain gifts that are not considered appropriate for giving to people who are hospitalized. These include potted plants and brightly colored cut flowers with strong scents. Also, it's only common sense that you shouldn't give any gifts of food products to people who are suffering from digestive ailments or need to restrict their intake of food.

For Fires or Other Disasters

Find out the level of damage and send a gift of money as soon as possible.

For Overseas Assignments

Generally, it's a good idea to give money. If you have selected a gift, make sure it is delivered before the person finishes packing to go overseas. Avoid giving any large or otherwise unwieldy gift at the airport before their departure.

On The Opening of a New Branch

Wall clocks or plants will be welcomed. Don't send wreaths or flowers because the contractor or building company most likely will send some.

For Company Trips, Parties and Other Activities

For best results, consult with the person in your client's company who will be responsible for the activity and determine either the amount of money or else the type of gifts you will donate. Donating prizes for company athletic competitions is popular.

Say "Thank You" in Writing

Presents that come to you at your office should always be opened at the office. If the gift is a confection or some other consumable product, it should be shared in the office when opened. No matter how clearly you may think the gift is intended for you, remember that it was addressed to you in your capacity as an employee of your company.

Sending a Thank-You

Send thank-you notes within three days of receiving the gift. The sooner you send them the better.

Thank-You Calls

Calling close relatives or friends to thank them for gifts is acceptable, but in business you must express your appreciation in writing.

Gifts that Don't Require a Return Gift

It's generally agreed that the following kinds of gifts don't require the giving of a gift in return: gifts on entering school or graduating, birthdays, gifts to celebrate a promotion, gifts received after a fire or other disaster, gifts from superiors during a hospitalization, seasonal gifts from subordinates or other lower-ranking people. Even though no return gift is required, however, the gift has to be acknowledged with a letter of thanks.

☛ Keep records of what you received and from whom. Send gifts of equal or greater value the next time the other person presents an appropriate occasion.

CHAPTER 7

FUNERALS

Attend All Work-Related Funerals

☛ When you hear about a client's death, report it through the proper channels so that no one will unknowingly show any discourtesy over the phone.

☛ Even when you attend the funeral as an individual, keep in mind that you represent the company. Be unfailingly polite.

☛ Use common sense in calculating how much to give in *Koden* (the money gifts given at funerals). Give as much as other companies.

☛ Send a wreath or other flower arrangement after asking the family's wishes.

☛ If you are called on to give a memorial address, work in some aspect of the deceased's life as a business person and save your condolences until the end.

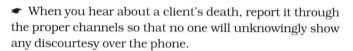

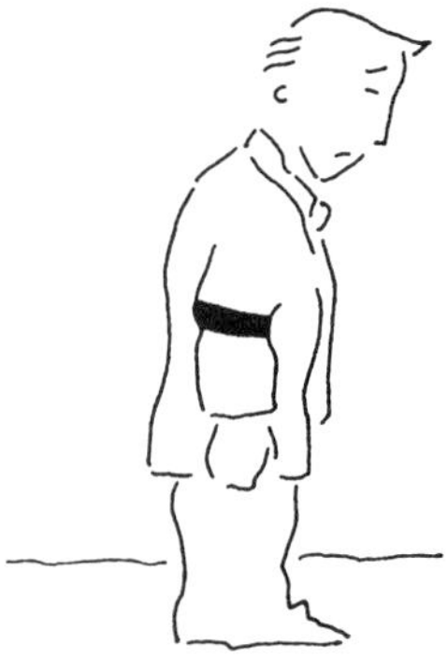

Attending a Customer's Funeral Comes Before All Else

A new employee at a securities house tells this story: "Late one night, I was working overtime when a call came in to inform us that the managing director of one of our client companies had just died in an accident. Since it was so late, I figured the best time to report it would be first thing the following morning. But the following morning, the boss was furious with me. No matter how late it is, you have to report that kind of news right away."

Depending on the rank of the customer, you may have to call an emergency meeting of all top executives. In such cases, ignorance of the situation is no excuse, and failure to act quickly can be embarrassing for the company.

Take Immediate Action

☛ If you send a telegram, decide whether it will be signed by the president or some other officer of the company.

☛ Will company people go to the wake? If so, who?

☛ How much will your company give in condolence money (*koden*)? Consult with other companies and give roughly the same amount.

☛ Will you send a wreath or some other type of floral arrangement? Will the flowers be sent in the name of the company or the president? It should be kept in mind that, lately, the sending of large wreaths is on the decline because they are felt to be merely advertising the company's name. At Christian funerals, it is customary not to attach cards or have the names of the giver conspicuously written on wreaths. In any case, consult with the family and observe their wishes.

☛ How many people from the company should attend the wake and funeral? Who? Who will be sent to help ?

☛ If you're asked to give a memorial address, prepare it quickly. Assemble materials and stories related to the life of the deceased and write the address with a writing brush.

Attending Funerals

☛ When you select those who will attend the funeral as representatives of the company, let the people coordinating the event know as soon as possible so they can plan seating and other matters.

☛ To the extent possible, have employees use public transportation to go to the funeral. Usually, the family will have to struggle just to get enough parking space for cars of close relatives.

☛ At the receiving line, express your condolence and sympathy to the family's representative. Then sign the condolence book, taking care to include your company's name and your section.

Most people will also leave a business card, with the lower left hand corner folded up in accordance with tradition.

What Would You Do?

On the death notice, it says the family declines to receive condolence money.

If you can't decide whether the family will actually refuse to accept money or just does not wish to look eager to receive it, prepare an envelope with the appropriate amount anyway, watch what others at the reception line do and act accordingly.

You arrive late.

If the person coordinating the receiving of mourners is still there, find him and make a profound apology. Then quietly find a seat in the last row of chairs set up for mourners. The next day, apologize to the family by telephone or in writing.

Neither you nor any other company representative can attend the funeral.

Mail a letter of condolence and the appropriate amount of condolence money to the family by registered mail.

Showing Extra Consideration

☛ The family, close friends and the chief mourner all must wear formal mourning clothes, but those attending on behalf of the company don't need to. At the wake, you should wear a dark suit, white shirt and an ordinary necktie. At the funeral or farewell service, you should wear a black or very dark suit, white shirt, black necktie and black shoes. Since the family of the deceased will be wearing black armbands there is no need for company representatives to.

☛ Strictly speaking, funeral services consist of three parts: the wake, the actual funeral and the farewell service for the deceased. It's traditional for the non-family member to attend the wake or the farewell service, while only family members attend the funeral itself. Farewell services are scheduled directly after the funeral, so take care to arrive in time.

☛ For those attending both wake and farewell service, there is no need to present condolence money twice.

☛ Express your condolences to the person in charge of receiving mourners. It's impolite to convey your sympathy directly to the family. When you offer incense to the memory of the departed and his family is nearby, you should bow to them but do not speak.

☛ When waiting in the receiving line at funeral services, remove your overcoat or shawl and drape it over your arm. Also, when waiting outside to see off the deceased's coffin, don't put your coat back on no matter how cold it is.

☛ If you run into someone you know at the funeral, acknowledge the person with your eyes only. Refrain from all conversation at services.

CHAPTER 8

COMPANY FUNERALS

- As soon as the news of an employee's death arrives, call a meeting of top management to decide if the company should conduct the funeral.
- If the deceased was influential in the business world, post a death notice in the newspapers.
- You can make a rough estimate of how many people will come to the funeral on the basis of the number of New Year's greeting cards the deceased sent in the previous year.
- Coordinate everything with the personnel of the funeral home so that the responsibility for each aspect of the service will be clearly defined.
- Employees will direct the cars at the event, but request the cooperation of the police in traffic control.
- The General Affairs Department will be the command center for the funeral. All employees of the department will be mobilized to assist in the effort.

Good Teamwork is Necessary

A Funeral is a Public Event

Use All Your Resources in Preparing for and Running It

Start Preparing as Soon as You Get the News

"We held a company funeral when our founder and chairman passed away," recalls Mr. K, the head of the general affairs department at a large steel maker. "As soon as he slipped into critical condition, we were forced to start making our

Keep in Mind

• Seating should be roughly classified into these categories: people related to the company, customers, friends. Mourners are to be seated in their order of arrival. Two exceptions: Those who had close ties to the deceased should be seated toward the center, and older people should be seated near the altars set up for the offering of incense.

• Important visitors who arrive late should not be seated in the last row, but rather should be shown to a waiting room for a short while. When the offering of incense begins, the VIP should be shown to the line of mourners waiting to approach the altar and allowed to go ahead of others in the line. If it's necessary to explain, tell those on line that he was a very close friend of the deceased.

preparations. First, we searched for an appropriate site to hold the funeral and then checked to see what days it would be available. Since the chairman also was a well-known public figure whose passing would be carried by all the news media, we put together an extended biography and a summary of his achievements to make answering inquiries easier. Since the head of the company is a public figure, the funeral takes on significance in society outside the company. To marshal the necessary resources to put on this type of public event, the company's system of routine in-house communication becomes all the more important."

After the chairman of the company died, Mr. K's department moved quickly:

☛ First an emergency top management meeting was called. The general affairs department then began assigning responsibility for each of the aspects of the funeral arrangements.

☛ Mr. K contacted the temple to which the chairman's family belonged to discuss the arrangements. It's the duty of the head of the general affairs department to have such information for the chairman and president of the company on file. It would be very embarrassing to have to go to the family in their time of bereavement to ask them for this information.

☛ Next the company made decisions on the time and place of each stage of the funeral services—the wake, the private family service and the main/farewell service.

☛ Mr. K knew it would be very difficult for all mourners to attend all services—the wake, the private service for the family, the main service and the farewell service. When circulating the memo on attendance to executives, he suggested which service each person should participate in.

☛ The general affairs department then made decisions on who to ask to be chief mourner, funeral coordinator, the representative for the deceased's friends and the speakers at the ceremonies. Mr. K then asked each to accept his roles.

☛ Mr. K's department selected newspapers in which the company would place death notices.

☛ The company then calculated the expected number of mourners. Mr. K advises that there are a variety of ways to do this: "You can come up with a good estimate based on either the number of New Year's greeting cards that came to the deceased's home each year, or the number of companies that pay official visits at the start of each year or the number of the company's stockholders."

Watch the Flow of Mourners at Services

At another company, they calculated there would be a maximum of 600 mourners. Estimating that between 120 and 150 people can offer incense for the repose of the departed's soul at a single altar, the company set up four altars for offering incense. The estimated 600 mourners were able to complete their offerings in a single hour.

But not all funerals go as planned. For example, there are times when far less than the expected number of mourners will come to the service. In such cases it's wise to remove some of the altars or the event will end too early, making it difficult to achieve the proper effect.

Mr. K advises again: "On the day of the funeral, the head of the general affairs department must check all aspects of the site without being too conspicuous. No matter what precautions you have taken, you should always assume there will be some sort of unanticipated problem."

If you learn in advance that more mourners than expected will come to the service, dispense with the incense and have people offer flowers instead. Incense offering takes more time. Only 2.5 people per minute can make incense offerings, in contrast to the 4-5 people a minute with offerings of flowers.

Success Depends on Smooth Teamwork

"Let the local police know in advance that you will hold a large service in their area, and give them the time, date and other details," Mr. K cautions. "They can give you good advice about parking near the site and may be able to set up some traffic control measures for you.

"On the day of the funeral, each person has to do his best in the area for which he is responsible. But don't get carried away. All staff should be aware that when setting up for the funeral, they shouldn't move any of the temple's property without getting permission.

"Be careful in handling the condolence money received. If you deposit it in one of the company's accounts and then give it to the family, the tax authorities will charge the family a gift tax. It's wise to deposit the money in one of the family's accounts as soon as it's collected."

- ***When many older mourners are expected for a funeral that will be held outdoors in very hot or very cold weather, prepare a waiting room with chairs and sofas that people can use if they begin to feel uncomfortable. In the winter, have lap warmers, hand warmers and blankets for older people to drape over their legs while seated outside.***

- ***Have all signs written by a good calligrapher to preserve the refined feeling of the event.***

- ***For the person in charge of reception and the recording secretaries, choose someone who can recognize the most important mourners by sight. Ask him to stay at his post and not move throughout the funeral. He can work closely with the people who are in charge of showing mourners to their seats.***

PART 5

A SHORT COURSE IN GENERAL AFFAIRS KNOW-HOW:

LEARN FROM THE PROS

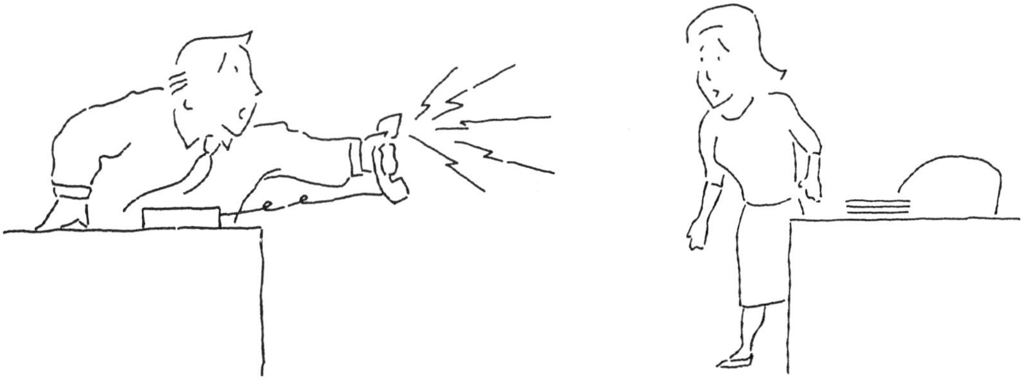

CHAPTER 1

CORPORATE STRUCTURE

Learn to See Things from the General Affairs Perspective

After All, It's Only Common Sense

We live in an age when a company's image and the trust it engenders have become standards for the selection of products. Without fostering a comprehensive image in the mind of the public, the company can no longer grow. For this reason, the sort of general affairs talent that can help to cultivate the corporate image is now very much in demand.

Companies with strong general affairs resources will grow, and business people with a clear general affairs perspective are being recognized as valuable corporate resources.

No matter how excellent a business person's achievements, he is a failure if he engages in activities that damage that public's trust in the company.

The Company from the General Affairs Standpoint

From the general affairs perspective, there are three basic areas of management: basic management, crisis management and service management. Mastery of these three management systems provides the infrastructure for the company's further development.

The general affairs department is where all of the company's various information is collected and processed. From it, you can see every move the company is making.

A General Affairs Spirit?

The senior manager in charge of general affairs at a securities company, Mr. W, discusses the characteristics of the general affairs personality: "General affairs people have to be able to get along with everyone: the top managers, the heads of each department and their people. In that sense, they're masters of *otsukiai*; they are always required to be in perfect control."

The general affairs person must almost have a mania for collecting and storing information on a wide variety of subjects: everything from a customer's financial condition to personnel changes, from a certain employee's state of mind to another's love life.

Again Mr. W speaks: "General affairs people should be energetic and fast on their feet. If you ask whether there are any conference rooms available for a meeting, they're the type that will pop up out of their seats immediately and take a look. They're able to talk with the same cheerfulness to anyone in the company, to find out what rumors are going around the company without damaging anyone's reputation. It's sometimes a thankless job, but if you can do it well, you'll be successful wherever you go in the company after that."

Acquiring Sensitivity

"The most important thing in a company," explains Mr. W, "is to secure a consensus before taking action. Whether it's a plan to cut company expenses or the implementation of office automation, to get the whole company moving together on an initiative, you have to stir up employee spirit. You can't just cram plans down their throats and think they'll accept them. This is where general affairs people's quick-wittedness and mastery of handling complicated matters can help.

"General affairs staff, however, can not be the type that craves acceptance by colleagues, or becomes easily dependent on others. If they are, then they'll favor certain departments or people instead of staying impartial. General affairs people should maintain moderation and distance when dealing with other employees."

As we move ahead into the Information Age, front-line business people will face the need for greater teamwork and will have to deal with a vastly larger set of complex human relationships. Companies must encourage their people to acquire the sensitivity, even tempers and quick wits of the general affairs person and use these resources effectively in their daily work.

CHAPTER 2

HANDLING COMPLAINTS

Passing the Buck is a Disgrace to the Company

Saying "I'm Sorry" on Behalf of the Company

What all companies that are ranked highly by the public have in common is a good relationship with consumers. Mr. H, the head of general affairs at a large brewing company, explains how his organization holds on to dissatisfied customers: "When we receive a call from a consumer complaining about a product, we take down the person's name and telephone number, get all the details about why the person is unhappy and then tell him or her that we'll get back to them. We don't transfer the call to someone else in the organization, because we don't want to waste more of the caller's time or money by keeping the person on the phone.

"We then contact our local representative in that area. He contacts the consumer directly the same day and makes arrangements to pay a call on him the following day. Our attitude is that even if it's only a minor complaint, we're the ones who are responsible for causing it. The customer took the trouble to look up our number and call us, so we have to do our best to handle the complaint."

Manufacturing companies devote an enormous amount of energy to seeing to it that complaints are resolved to the consumers' satisfaction. This same spirit can be used with success in every line of business.

What Does the Person Want?

Mr. K, an insurance company executive, realizes now that handling complaints promptly can build good will for the company: "We had a dozen bottles of juice delivered to us in a carton, and one of the bottles was leaking. I called to complain about it and the same day, a representative brought replacements, not only for the bottle that was broken but for two others that were covered with juice. I was very impressed that they took so much care about a single bottle of their product, and my impression of their company improved all the more. There are many companies that will exchange unsatisfactory products but, unfortunately, a good number do it only reluctantly. You should always keep in mind that handling complaints is an expensive process, and take steps to see to it that complaints are kept at a minimum."

People complain for a variety of reasons. Some want their product replaced, others want it repaired. Still others demand an apology and a show of sincerity along with a replacement product.

Again, brewing company executive Mr. H speaks: "From a single phone call, a veteran in consumer affairs can tell more or less what the person with the complaint wants." After his company receives a complaint, it notifies the local representative and asks him to take action on the matter. At the same time, the company tells the representative whether there is reason to give the matter "rush" handling, specifies the nature of the complaint and gives a little background information on the consumer. Providing sufficient documents and other materials is the duty of the person who receives the complaint, and provides a quick way to come to a satisfactory solution with the complaining consumer.

Handling Complaints by the Book

☛ When receiving complaints, or when it's necessary to apologize, do so as a representative of the company. Always listen to the person's complaint fully.

☛ If it appears that your company is at fault and the caller has said that he or she is calling long distance, offer to hang up and call the person back. This tells the person with a legitimate complaint

Use the Telephone Effectively

Mr. M, a general manager in an audio equipment manufacturing company, tells how he uses telephone technology to help him handle complaints: "Today's telephones really make things simple. For example, I can put a dissatisfied consumer on hold while I call the factory in Hiroshima to consult on the problem. Also, I like to make use of the speakerphone so that my subordinates can hear the details and get in touch with the appropriate sections of the company right away to deal with the problem. While they're consulting with the factory or other departments, I ask the consumer where the product was bought and other such information. In this way, we get a lot of very valuable data."

that your company is sincere about wanting to provide a satisfactory solution to the problem. It also discourages those who call out of boredom or malice, since by letting you know their phone number, you can find out where they live.

☛ If the complaint is an extremely simple one and you're sure that someone in your office can handle it promptly, put the caller on hold and transfer the call to that person.

☛ The first requirement in handling complaints is speed. The system has to be such that even if the person in charge of taking care of such matters is out of the office, there will be no disruption in the proper handling of each matter. Cooperation among different sections of the company in handling such matters must be continuously improved. Good communications between repair shops and affiliated companies involved in handling complaints are also vital.

☛ Just because you've finished processing a complaint, don't just forget about the matter. Make a record of it and report it to the appropriate section of the company. A complaint that's made to your company should be treated as valuable "living" data from the public. Along with its value in preventing a future outbreak of complaints, it can also be useful in discussing how to improve old products or discussing new ones.

For Those Who Don't Like Handling Complaints

Here are a few examples of how complaints led to business successes:

☛ A life insurance sales person went to settle a claim against the company on a holiday. The customer appreciated his sincerity and agreed to buy another policy from him.

☛ "Why do rice cookers open toward the right?" one caller asked an electronics maker's customer affairs department. She suggested that if the appliance opened the other way, it would be more convenient to right-handed people. This sort of valuable information can come out of complaints.

Complaints can be a treasure trove of important business information and good business opportunities. Take on complaints aggressively, and never forget that, as a business person, everything you do will reflect on your company.

5

CHAPTER 3

THE OFFICE ENVIRONMENT

Cleanliness and Trust

The Proper Office Layout for the People Working There

Everyone would prefer to work in an office that looks like an office automation equipment manufacturer's showroom. Unfortunately, the reality in which we work is far different.

Smokers Versus Non-Smokers

Smoking in the office is annoying to those who don't smoke. Of course, there is often no way to divide up the office to prevent this, but to the extent possible, smokers should be separated from non-smokers. You can also make sure that ventilators and other passages where air flows are not blocked by large cabinets or other office equipment. It's also wise to install air-purifying equipment.

Meetings Disrupt the Pace of Work

In offices where meeting rooms are next to workspaces, noisy meetings sometimes distract employees from their work. In such cases, it's sometimes effective to create cubicles with panels that are about 1.5 meters high. If the person stands he can see the whole office, but once seated has a more private work environment.

☛ Desks for the boss and his subordinates shouldn't be too close.

☛ All filing cabinets should be within five meters of the person's desk.

☛ The space between people's desks depends on the work that they are doing:

- 75-120 cm for people working together as a team
- 120-210 cm for people working on their own projects as well as group projects
- 210-360 cm for people who need to concentrate wholly on their own projects

To Work Together Smoothly

Even when you have introduced office automation, it's still a good idea to go over your office layout with a critical eye to see if it's contributing to improved productivity.

☛ Are files and other documents located where they are easily accessible? Is there space for someone to stand and look at them without getting in someone else's way?

☛ Are faxes delivered right away to the person they're addressed to?

☛ Is there enough space near the copiers to sort and collate copies?

☛ Working at word processors or other computer terminals can lead to vision problems and backaches. Use properly designed chairs and lighting to reduce such problems.

☛ Are piles of useless documents taking up a lot of space in the office? Everyone should keep their desks and the area around them neat and clean.

☛ Do you have a bulletin board that shows everyone's daily schedule in a highly visible place?

Are You Conscious of Office Management?

Mr. T, a manager in the office of the chief executive officer of a large securities company, tries to get his subordinates to cut down on waste: "One woman in our office fills a pot up with boiling water to brew a single cup of tea. Then she throws the rest away. That sort of waste adds up and damages the company."

Mr. S, a general manager at a fuel oil company, offers another example: "I'll ask someone to make 10 copies of a document for me, and he or she will just go to the copier, put the document on the platen and run off ten copies. Now, if they didn't copy well, that's ten copies wasted. What the person should do is make one sample copy to see how well the document copies, and if it's satisfactory make nine more. It seems some people just don't understand how hard it is for a company to squeeze out even an extra 10,000 yen in after-tax net profits."

Key points to check in campaigns to reduce office expenses include the following:

☛ Are the purchases of office machines and supplies necessary? Do other departments or sections have more of those items than they can use?

☛ Create a logbook to keep track of office machines and supplies. Someone should be appointed to be responsible for important office machines.

☛ Each month employees should check their desk drawers to see if they have more office supplies than they need. If they do, they should return the excess to the office manager.

If employees understand that cost reduction is linked to increasing company profits, they can't very well complain about management carrying things too far.

Be Serious about Cleanliness

People somehow are more likely to trust a company whose offices are clean. Keep an eye out for trouble spots. If cleaning chores rotate among employees, make sure it's understood that such tasks are also part of the job.

CHAPTER 4

SAFETY

Everyone Should Be Alert

Don't Leave Things in the Halls — Keep an Eye on the Roof and Parking Lot

Department store manager Mr. I recalls how he became more safety conscious: "A product display case fell over and one of our customers was cut by the glass. Luckily, his injuries weren't severe, but I shudder when I think that the accident could have permanently damaged his health, or worse."

The first step towards workplace safety starts with changing structural plans and other layouts that present dangers to people. Beware of tables and chairs that have sharply pointed corners. Tall bookshelves are easily tipped over unless they are firmly secured to the wall.

If a suicide leaps from your company's roof or there is a brawl in your parking lot, it damages the confidence the public has in your company. Take care that the roof and parking lot are kept under observation. Make each employee conscious of the need to be alert for potentially dangerous situations, and they will be able to take quick action to report the problem. Employees can also make valuable suggestions on how to improve safety.

87% of All Crimes are Thefts — Don't Leave a Thief Any Opportunities

Today's thief wears a smart-looking suit and tie. He only aims for cash, and needs under ten minutes to get it. His main goal is to avoid being caught, so he'll never go near places that display a sticker showing you participate in a crime prevention program organized by the local police department.

There are also many purse snatchers who lie in wait for the unsuspecting person returning from the bank on payday or during bonus season. Employees who take cash home on such days should walk together and should hold their shoulder bags tightly, and keep them in front of them.

Make It a Rule

☛ All valuables, contracts and other important documents should be placed in the company's safe deposit box.

☛ Improve relations with the local police and show a willingness to cooperate with them. It will help to heighten your employees' consciousness of crime prevention if you seek the guidance of the police from time to time.

☛ Strictly control access to office keys used by employees for overtime work, and make them conscious of the need to cooperate to prevent crimes. Appoint someone who will be responsible for controlling the use of keys, and always be aware of the number of keys that are in use.

☛ Participate actively in all crime prevention programs, fire drills, and disaster training exercises.

☛ Learn how to employ alarms and closed-circuit television monitoring to combat crime.

PART 6

AN ILLUSTRATED GUIDE TO OTSUKIAI

CHAPTER 1

SEATING ARRANGEMENTS FOR ENTERTAINING GUESTS

Seating Protocol

When guest and host are both vying to offer one another the best seat, one should make a point of not being too insistent. For entertaining in a traditional Japanese room, no one should be seated until all members of the party are present. If there is no room for waiting, the host(s) should sit in the less desirable positions and wait for the guest or guests to arrive. The main guest should be seated with his back to the Tokonoma.

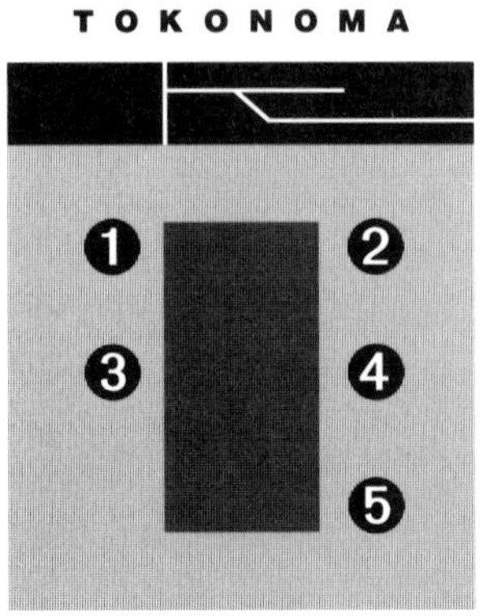

Tokonoma

The traditional Japanese house has a room with an alcove (Tokonoma), in which are displayed decorative elements meant to create a relaxing atmosphere. In this room, the most important guest is seated with his or her back to the Tokonoma.

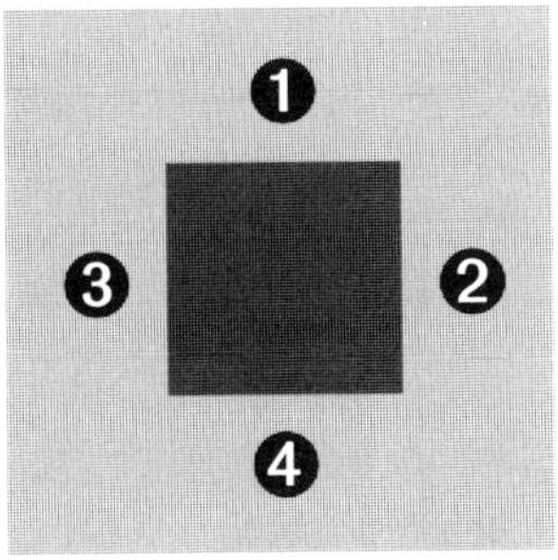

In a Restaurant

The most important guest takes the seat farthest from the entrance.

In a Chinese Restaurant

The most important guest is again seated farthest from the entrance. The host should sit directly opposite this guest.

French-style Vs. British-style Seating

If there are female guests in attendance (or when couples are invited), the seating of male and female members at formal dinners should be alternated. If the group is all-male, and the party lacks a hostess, the second-ranking host person should assume the role of hostess.

French ***British***

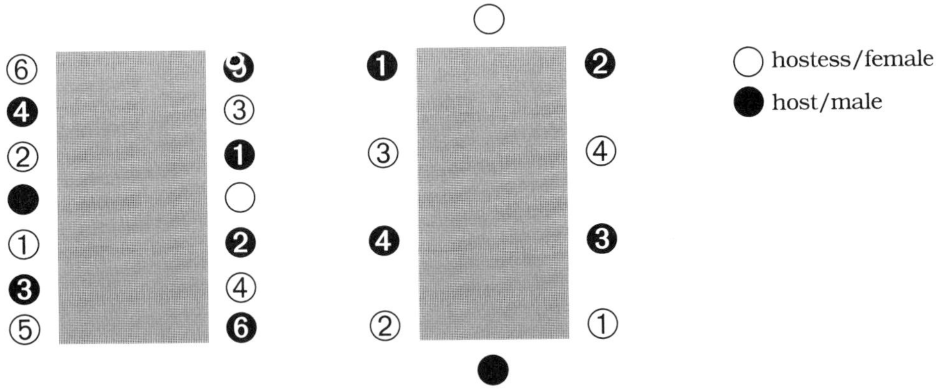

CHAPTER 2

ESCORTING YOUR GUEST

Some Useful Tips

In Hallways

Lead your guest, a step or two ahead, staying to his left or right, rather than walking directly in front of him.

In Elevators

You should be the first to enter the elevator and press the button for the desired floor. When the elevator doors open, let your guests off first.

Stairs

In stairways, always lead your guest when you are going up the steps, and remain behind your guest when going down.

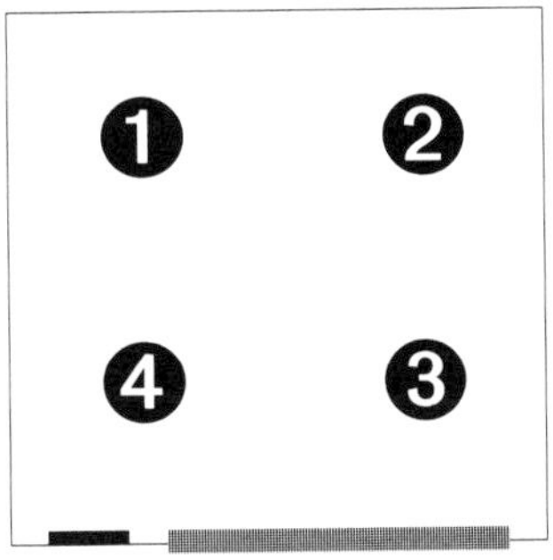

Elevators

The best position for the most important guest is at the rear of the elevator car. The least desirable position is next to the control panel.

At an Entrance

When the door opens inward (away from you), you should enter first and hold it for your guest. When the door opens outward (towards you), open it and hold it for your guest.

CHAPTER 3

SEATING ARRANGEMENTS FOR CONFERENCES AND MEETINGS

General Conference

U-Shaped Table

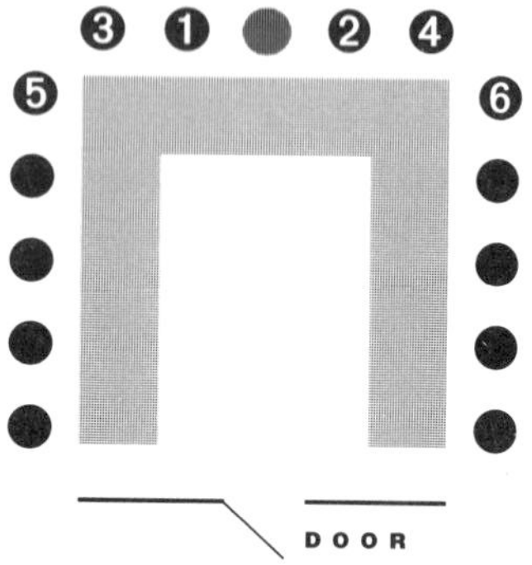

Square Table

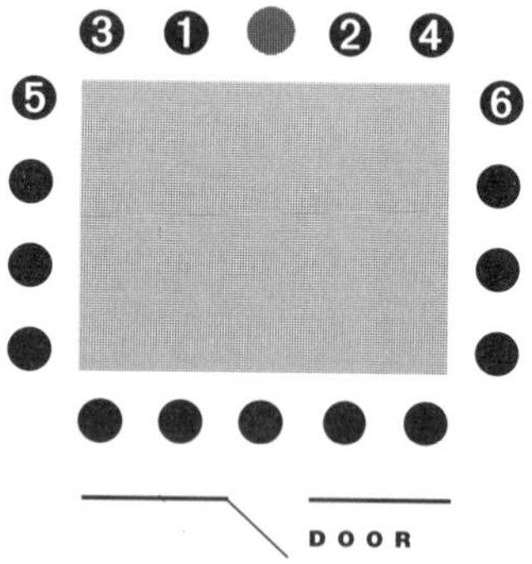

Smaller Meetings

With Host/Chairperson

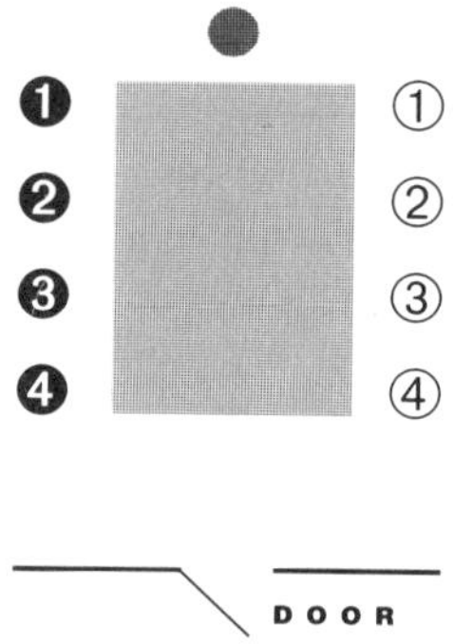

Without Host/Chairperson

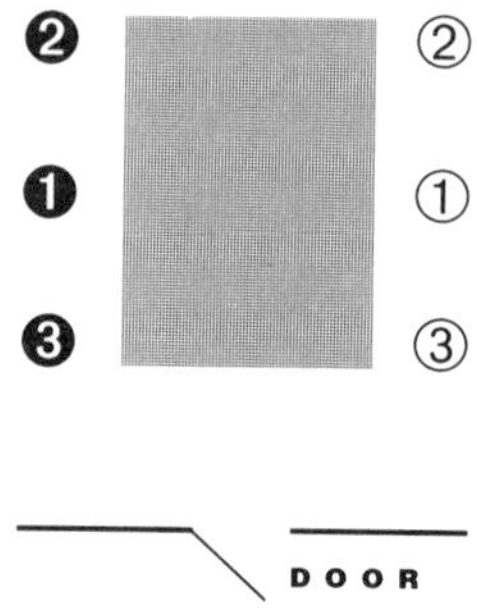

Receiving Visitors

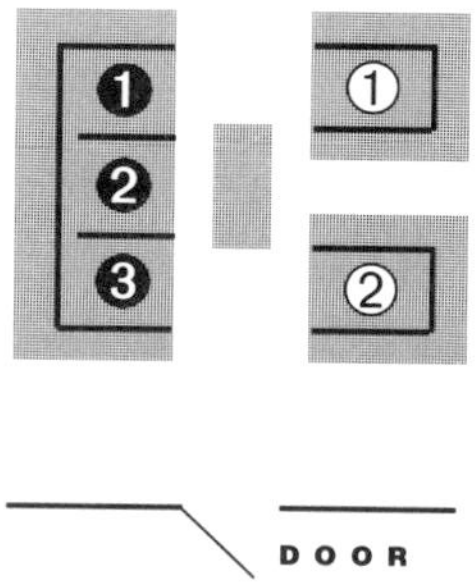

Round Table

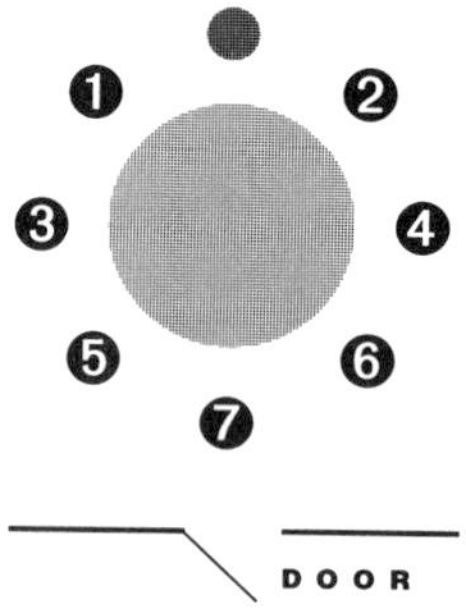

● host/chairperson

● guests

○ your company

CHAPTER 4

TRANSPORTATION SEATING

In Cars

If the vehicle is chauffeured, the seat directly behind the driver is for the most important person.

In seating the rest of the party, the order is as follows: after the first guest, the second most important person should occupy the other rear window seat, with the third taking the seat in between.

The fourth seat, next to the driver, is for the host.

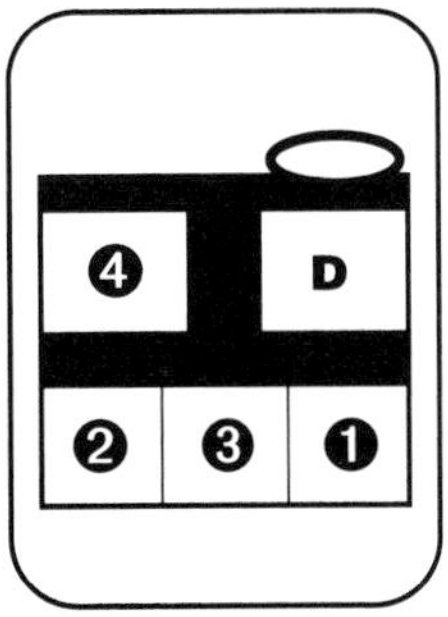

If you are driving, the seat next to the driver is most appropriate for the most important guest, the rear right window seat is next. The center rear is the least desirable.

Take care to give special attention to ladies or handicapped people among the guests.

Window seats should be provided for them.

Car Doors

When getting into or out of cars, hold the door open to help the most important guest.

On Trains

The most important guest(s) should be seated next to the window, preferably facing forward in the direction in which the train is moving. Again, the middle seats are the ones which are considered the least desirable.

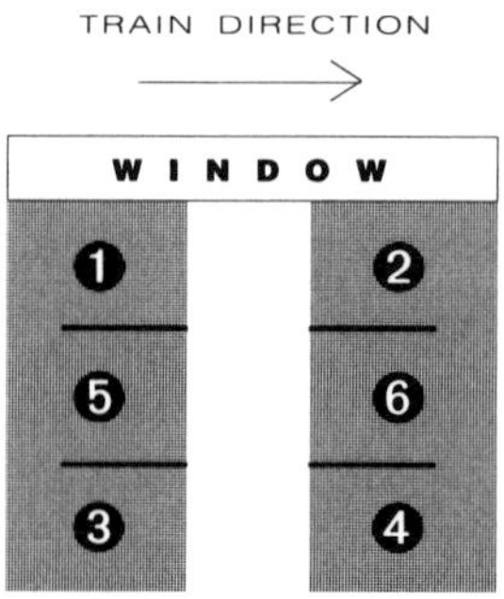

CHAPTER 5

TRADITIONAL CEREMONIES

Here is the basic flow of events generally found in Shinto ceremonies:

1. Purification rites (to dispel bad fortune or evil influences)
2. Making offerings to Shinto gods
3. Summoning the gods (the priest faces the altar and calls the gods down to earth)
4. Congratulatory addresses
5. Offering of branches from the *sakaki* (cleyera ochnacea), a tree considered sacred
6. Other rites may follow, including ground-breaking ceremonies
7. Bidding the gods to return from earth

A Short Guide to Behavior at Shinto Ceremonies

Purification Rites

The priest holds a branch of the *sakaki*, or cutting of silk and paper attached to a branch, and waves it three times over the head of each person being purified. Keep your head bowed until you hear the sound of the priest waving the *sakaki* branch over your head for until third time, then raise it.

Congratulatory Addresses

When the priest begins to read the congratulatory address, bow your head. When he stops reading, raise your head. (This also applies to ceremonies 3 and 7 listed in the box on page 180.)

Offering Sakaki Branches

1. Receive the branch from the priest and bow. Holding the stem in your right hand and the leafy part in your left, raise the branch to chest level to make the offering.

2. Stop two to three steps in front of the altar, raise the branch to eye level and bow.

3. Turning the branch with the flat of the palm of the left hand, make a circular motion with it. Switch the position of the hands so that the base of the branch is pointed toward the altar and then lay it on the altar as an offering.

4. Bow twice, clap twice and then bow again.

5. Take several steps backward, bow to the priest and then return to your seat.

(In abbreviated ceremonies, you can dispense with the *sakaki* branches and just pray.)

Offering of Incense and Flowers at Funerals and MemorialServices

Offering Incense from a Standing Position

1. When your turn comes, take a step forward and bow to the family of deceased and the Buddhist priest conducting the service.

2. About three to four steps from the altar with the incense burner, bow once to the spirit of the deceased, then advance to the altar and bring your palms together in prayer.

3. Grasp a piece of incense with the thumb, pointer and middle finger of the right hand, raise it to eye level, then drop it into the incense burner.

4. Join your palms again and then take three to four steps backwards, turn to the family and the priest, bow and then return to your seat.

Offering Incense from a Seated Position

1. Take a seated position in front of the family and priest, then bow.

2. Approach the altar and bow very deeply at the edge of the cushion placed before it.

3. Seated, kneeling on the cushion, take a piece of incense, raise it to eye level as an offering to the departed, then drop it carefully into the incense burner.

4. Join your palms together in prayer. Then, turn around on your knees and bow to the family and priest. Afterwards, stand and leave the altar.

Offering Incense Sticks

1. Sit kneeling before the incense burner on the altar, then bow, facing the family and priest. After joining your hands in prayer to the deceased, take a stick of incense in your right hand and light it, using the candle on the altar.

2. Once the incense stick is lit, gently extinguish the flame by fanning your left hand in front of it.

3. Place your incense in the burner, a little away from the others already burning there.

4. Join your palms together in prayer, leave the cushion and bow to the family and priest.

6

Offering Flowers

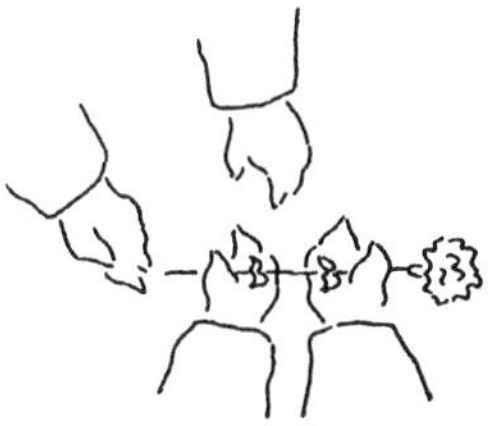

1. Accept the flower so that the bloom is to your right, with the stem to your left, then bow to picture of the deceased.

2. Raise the flower to chest level to offer it to the deceased, then approach the altar set up to receive the flowers and bow.

3. Turn the flower, so that the bloom faces you and place it on the altar.

4. Bow once more to the picture of the deceased and offer a silent prayer.